THE SMALL GUIDE TO DEPRESSION

THE SMALL GUIDE TO DEPRESSION

GARY SMALL, MD, AND GIGI VORGAN

Humanix Books
www.humanixbooks.com

Humanix Books

The Small Guide to Depression
Copyright © 2021 by Humanix Books
All rights reserved

Humanix Books, P.O. Box 20989, West Palm Beach, FL 33416, USA
www.humanixbooks.com | info@humanixbooks.com

Humanix Books is a division of Humanix Publishing, LLC. Its trademark, consisting of the words "Humanix" is registered in the Patent and Trademark Office and in other countries.

Disclaimer: The information presented in this book is not specific medical advice for any individual and should not substitute medical advice from a health professional. If you have (or think you may have) a medical problem, speak to your doctor or a health professional immediately about your risk and possible treatments. Do not engage in any care or treatment without consulting a medical professional.

ISBN: 978-1-63006-159-3 (Hardcover)
ISBN: 978-1-63006-160-9 (E-book)

Printed in the United States of America
10   9   8   7   6   5   4   3   2   1

Contents

Preface

ALMOST EVERYONE HAS FELT depressed over something in their lives—a loss, a breakup, missing out on a great sale—but occasionally feeling depressed is not the same thing as being depressed. It's normal for our mood to vary according to what we're thinking, feeling, and experiencing at any given time. However, fluctuations in mood and short-lived emotional responses to life challenges can sometimes make it difficult to differentiate between normal reactions to events and a case of clinical depression.

At some point, approximately one in five people will experience depression serious enough to require treatment from a medical professional. This disorder not only limits one's productivity and interferes with relationships; it can diminish quality of life and reduce life expectancy.

The World Health Organization reported in 2017 that over 264 million people around the world

suffered from depression. That same year, the
National Survey on Drug Use and Health estimated
that 7 percent of all adults in the US had experienced
a major depressive episode in the past twelve months.
Depression increases a person's risk for suicide, and
in 2018, nearly fifty thousand Americans died due to
suicide. Suicide is the second leading cause of death
in individuals between the ages of thirty-five and
fifty-four.

The COVID-19 pandemic escalated symptoms
of depression, and according to a 2020 American
Psychiatric Association survey, about one-third of
Americans felt that the pandemic was having a serious impact on their mental health, and nearly 60 percent reported feeling that coronavirus was seriously
impacting their daily lives. Fear, widespread anxiety,
economic downturn, and other sources of stress had
a negative psychological impact on people around the
world and exacerbated impairments for those already
suffering from mental illness. The measures taken to
slow the spread of the virus, such as social distancing,
business and school closures, and shelter-in-place
orders, led to greater isolation and stress—both risk
factors for developing depression.

In addition to stress from life crises that trigger
symptoms of depression, everyday worries, disappointments, health issues, financial instability,
relationship problems, and more can worsen mood
symptoms. And each of us has a genetic and innate

biological risk profile that contributes to the likelihood of getting depressed.

This book will help you understand your innate
risk factors and external triggers for developing
depression. It will show you how to distinguish
between normal emotional responses to life events
and more extreme forms of ongoing sadness that
interfere with daily function and do not improve on
their own, better known as clinical depression. You
will be able to gauge whether your feelings of sadness
are normal and appropriate or whether you could
benefit from some help—from a mental health professional, from taking advantage of the do-it-yourself
techniques described in this book, or from a combination of the two. Taking action to reduce your
depression will not only improve your well-being and
brain health; it will also reduce your risk for physical
illnesses and help you live longer and better.

CHAPTER 1

What Is Depression and Do You Have It?

Depression is merely anger without enthusiasm.
—Steven Wright

ROB JOGGED FIVE MILES a day since college and hardly missed a day in the thirty years since. He loved how it lifted his mood—which helped him put up with his overdemanding boss. It seemed like no matter how hard he worked, it was never enough. Sometimes he felt hopeless and out of control of his life, but his daily runs helped keep him sane.

On a particularly tough day at work, he couldn't wait to get home, lace up his running shoes, and hit the asphalt. He knew it would clear his head and help him brush off the insults he'd stomached that day. As Rob started jogging, he continued to seethe over things he wished he would have said to his boss. Just as he turned a corner, Rob's right foot caught a pot-hole and he twisted his ankle, falling to the ground in pain. Luckily, Rob was only two blocks from home, and he managed to limp back on his rapidly swelling ankle.

Rob's wife took him to urgent care, where the X-ray showed no break. The doctor wrapped his ankle, gave him an ice pack, and told him to rest for the next four to six weeks—no jogging.

Rob had sprained his ankle before, but it never hurt this bad and that scared him. What if he could never jog again? Rob took three days off from work, couldn't even concentrate enough to watch TV, and stayed home and moped. Every helpful suggestion his wife made pissed him off, and Rob found himself becoming weepy for no reason.

Back at work, Rob had to force himself to concentrate and nearly blew his top at his boss several times. He had little appetite, couldn't sleep past four each morning, and was tired all the time. During one of his sleepless nights, it occurred to him that his ankle would never be the same and his life as he knew it was over.

* * * * *

All of us experience sad feelings from time to time. It's impossible to go through life without disappointments, mishaps, and frustrations that get us down. Before his jogging accident, Rob certainly had daily irritations he had to deal with but he managed to avoid blowing up at his boss and losing his job. He was able to cope with those feelings through his exercise. His resulting endorphin high helped him avoid more serious mood changes.

But once Rob sprained his ankle and could no longer get in his daily jog, his mild depressive feelings morphed into a more serious episode of depression that truly disrupted his life. In fact, he suffered from many of the features of major depression, including a decline in appetite, insomnia, impaired concentration, feelings of hopelessness, irritability, and low energy levels.

When someone experiences a clinical depression, it is almost as if they are viewing the world through gray-tinted glasses. The cup shifts from being half full to half empty. Rob worried that his ankle would never heel, and he blamed himself—if he had only spotted the pothole, he could have avoided the accident. Psychiatrists sometimes refer to depression as being anger turned against oneself. Many depressed people like Rob are seething with anger that is manifested by feelings of guilt (turned against the self) and irritability (turned against others).

Some people describe depression as feeling like they continually have a black cloud over their heads. They have trouble getting out of bed, completing any task, or even wanting to do anything at all. They turn inward and avoid others, which only makes their situation worse. Getting outside and interacting with people, especially those who are not suffering from depression, can help distract someone who is sad from their negative ruminations.

Even though depression is considered a mental disorder, it can truly feel physical. Like other depressed individuals, Rob had physical symptoms—insomnia, loss of appetite, and fatigue. The physical and emotional symptoms that characterize clinical depression can become so excruciating that, left untreated, can cause the patient's life to become severely restricted and intolerable, and the condition can be life threatening. Multiple studies indicate that people who suffer from clinical or even milder depressions have a twofold greater risk of dying than those who are not depressed.

Despite the devastating impact of depression on people's lives, effective treatments are available. Various forms of psychotherapy, antidepressant medications, or both have been shown to work, and many patients can remain depression-free for years or for the rest of their lives. Many nonmedical interventions are effective as well. Rob's daily habit of jogging was a lifestyle choice that held his depressive tendencies at bay, and numerous studies have demonstrated how higher levels of daily physical activity have significant effects on lifting mood. Even going on a weight-loss diet can improve mood and lift feelings of sadness.

But before people can get help for depression, they first need to realize that they are suffering from the symptoms. The clinical symptoms of depression, whether it is a mild condition or one requiring medical intervention, can be recognized and identified. This is the first step to getting the help that can bring depression sufferers back to a productive and fulfilling life.

The bottom line is that depression is highly treatable. And although several successful medical interventions, lifestyle strategies, and alternative therapies are available, currently only about one out of every three sufferers receive proper treatment.

THE DEPRESSION EPIDEMIC

Most of us are aware of the common major diseases like heart disease, diabetes, cancer, and others that impair everyday living and can be lethal. However, major mental illnesses like depression are often overlooked or ignored and can be just as lethal and life-damaging as any physical condition.

Epidemiological studies indicate that the rate of symptoms of depression and clinical depression has been increasing during the past several decades throughout the world. The lifetime prevalence of depression (i.e., the rate of developing depression at any point in life) ranges from 20 to 25 percent in women and 7 to 12 percent in men.

Nearly 8 percent of Americans age twelve years or older suffer from moderate to severe depression.

ARE YOU DEPRESSED?

To get an idea of whether someone is suffering from mild, moderate, or more severe symptoms of depression, mental health professionals often ask patients to complete a self-rating questionnaire. Below are twenty symptoms of depression that appear in many of these surveys. Check off any symptom(s) that you may be feeling now or have felt in the last few weeks and then tally the number of symptoms you endorsed. If you checked more than six items, there is a good chance that you are experiencing some form of depression and could benefit from many of the strategies described in this book.

- ☐ Difficulty sleeping at night
- ☐ Tearfulness or feeling like crying
- ☐ Poor appetite
- ☐ Feeling sad or blue for two weeks or more
- ☐ Decreased libido
- ☐ Feeling worse in the morning
- ☐ Weight loss
- ☐ Constipation
- ☐ Rapid heartbeat at times
- ☐ Fatigue for no reason
- ☐ Not thinking clearly
- ☐ Difficulty getting things done

☐   Restlessness

☐   Hopelessness

☐   Feeling of guilt or letting people down

☐   Indecisiveness

☐   Feelings of uselessness

☐   Lack of interest in things one previously enjoyed

☐   Feeling that life is not worth living

☐   Irritability

Total number of items checked: _____

That proportion rises to 10 percent for people aged forty to fifty-nine. If left unchecked, severe forms of depression can be silent killers. The most direct cause of death due to depression is suicide, and depression is the most common cause of suicidal thinking and behavior. For those aged fifteen to thirty-four years, suicide is the second most common cause of death.

Depression is also a major cause of absenteeism from work and can increase the risk of many other health problems ranging from diabetes to stroke disease or dementia. Having depression increases the chances of developing a cardiac disease by 50 percent and also raises the risk of fatal heart attacks.

The close link between depression and physical illness is reflected in the high rates of depression in outpatient clinics. A recent meta-analysis of several epidemiological studies indicated that 27 percent of people visiting outpatient clinics have a clinical depression or depressive symptoms, with a range of 17 to 53 percent depending on the particular clinical department. Ear, nose, and throat patients experienced the highest prevalence of depression (53 percent) followed by dermatology patients (39 percent).

DID YOU KNOW?

People who are depressed sometimes have problems regulating their body temperature, or what is known as an altered thermoregulatory system. Dr. Charles Raison of the University of Wisconsin in Madison, Wisconsin, and collaborators found that exposing the entire body to heat may be a safe and rapid way to improve mood in people who are depressed. That may be why many people notice a lift in their mood after doing hot yoga or spending time in a warm bath or shower, sauna, or hot tub.

WHAT'S THE DIFFERENCE BETWEEN
SADNESS AND DEPRESSION?

Many people use the words *sad* and *depressed* interchangeably. Feeling sad is a major aspect of depression, but they are not the same thing, and knowing how they differ is helpful in understanding how to deal with mood symptoms.

Feeling sad from time to time is a normal human experience. Many everyday events can induce sadness. Losses are common triggers for such unhappy feelings, and they can come in the form of a divorce, absence of a loved one, losing a job, getting demoted at work, failing an exam, or any form of disappointment or stress. When someone feels sad, however, they are usually able to experience relief from the feelings by talking to a friend, crying, or getting some exercise. Sadness usually has an identifiable trigger. Moreover, the sad feelings go away on their own over time.

If sad feelings do not pass with time or they interfere with a person's ability to function normally in life, that could be a signal that they are suffering from depression—a mental disorder can feel overpowering and can severely impact a person's life. Although depression can be triggered by stress or loss, sometimes it has no obvious cause.

People who are depressed often experience other accompanying symptoms, such as feelings of discouragement, hopelessness, low motivation, poor concentration abilities, and a loss of interest in their usual activities that were once enjoyable. Physical symptoms such as insomnia, weight loss or gain, and fatigue are also common with depression. Depressed people sometimes become so discouraged that they feel that suicide is the only way out. If such symptoms last more than two weeks, the individual may be experiencing an episode of major depression or some other type of depressive disorder.

WHY AM I SO SAD?

Sometimes we feel sad and we are not sure why. No single cause can explain the many forms of sadness, but past experiences and genetic predispositions will determine each individual's risk for developing a depressive disorder. These factors have an impact on our brain chemistry, personality style, and tolerance for stress, which ultimately determine who will develop normal, mild depressive symptoms or a full-blown disorder.

If one of your parents has or had a history of depressive symptoms or suffered from a mood disorder, your own risk increases two- to threefold. For the average person, genetic inheritance accounts for approximately 40 percent of the risk for a depressive disorder.

In addition to passing on their DNA or genetic material to us, our parents' behavior impacts our ability to cope and adapt to depressing situations beginning at a very young age. Whether our parents modeled healthy responses to stress or taught us their own unhealthy emotional reactions will shape our own coping ability and temperament. A person whose personality is rigid, volatile, pessimistic, or insecure will likely have greater difficulty managing their mood than a more resilient, optimistic, and self-confident individual.

Physical illnesses and medication side effects can also lead to symptoms of depression. For instance, patients with diabetes who take too much insulin will often experience acute mood changes from a sudden drop in their blood sugar.

Sometimes depression symptoms are directly caused by a physical illness. For example, our bodies need normal levels of thyroid hormones to run smoothly. If those levels get too low, hypothyroidism occurs, which may then lead to fatigue, forgetfulness, and depression. As a result, hypothyroidism can be mistaken for depression. Many other illnesses ranging from diabetes to heart disease can lead to depression. Also, heavy coffee drinkers may experience fatigue and other mood symptoms when their caffeine levels get too low, often before their first cup in the morning.

COMMON SOURCES OF DEPRESSION

- Stress from work or school

- Interpersonal relationship problems

- Financial pressure

- Medical illnesses

- Medication side effects

- Emotional trauma

- Death of a loved one

- Recreational drugs

- Isolation and loneliness

If you are a woman, you are twice as likely to suffer from depression than if you are a man. Your age will influence your risk as well. Symptoms of clinical depression increase as people age, and this is especially true for women.

It's also true that as we get older, we experience different forms of depression. A majority of older people develop chronic physical illnesses, which can trigger considerable emotional reactions. Older people may focus on their physical ailments and concentration difficulties, which can actually be depression presenting itself as a physical or cognitive illness.

DID YOU KNOW?

The bacteria in your intestine may be causing your depression. Recent research on the trillions of bacteria that live in your gut suggests that dietary adjustments that include probiotics and prebiotics could possibly lift your mood.

THE DEPRESSED BRAIN

Several brain areas are involved in controlling our emotional responses. The amygdala, a tiny region that resides beneath the temples of the forehead, serves to regulate our feelings of sadness and despair. The amygdala is part of the limbic system, a group of structures deep in the brain associated with many emotions that often emerge in people who are depressed, including anger, hopelessness, and sorrow. Abnormalities in the structure and function of these brain regions have been identified in people who are depressed.

Depressed people often have faulty connections between their amygdalae and other brain regions that control mood during a depressive episode. These faulty connections are thought to contribute to difficulties controlling mood, leading to irritability, anger, and intense temper outbursts. The hippocampus, which resides near the amygdala, converts

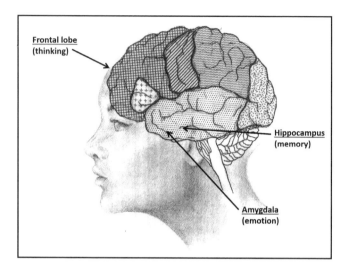

these negative emotional experiences into long-term memories.

Another brain region activated by mood changes is the frontal lobe, also called the "thinking brain." This part of the brain processes uncomfortable emotions and attempts to put them into perspective. Sometimes intense feelings of sadness can overload the frontal lobe's capacity to regulate emotional responses.

Chronic or even intermittent stress can cause wear and tear on the brain regions that control our emotional responses. For example, research indicates that the hippocampus is actually smaller in people who were abused as children or were in military combat.

DID YOU KNOW?

People with a neurotic personality style have a tendency to experience irritability, anger, sadness, worry, and self-doubt. Their neuroticism increases their risk for developing symptoms of depression. However, IQ may have a protective effect against depression in some situations. Multiple studies suggest that higher levels of intelligence protect against the likelihood that neurotic personality traits will lead to symptoms of depression.

SOCIAL MEDIA AND DEPRESSION

In recent years, advances in technology have made it easy to communicate and transmit information rapidly, which has enhanced our efficiencies at work and at home. The internet and twenty-four-hour news cycle can inform and connect us, but the persistent flow of information can become exhausting and increase mood instability.

Social media platforms like Twitter, Facebook, Instagram, and Snapchat have become a dominant presence in our lives and provide a conduit for sharing our experiences with others. But for many people who are prone to feelings of depression, these platforms can become an unrelenting form of peer pressure—a need to be better, happier, richer, and more successful than the others on our friends list.

For young people, particularly adolescents and twentysomethings, when the susceptibility to peer pressure and the desire to conform with friends is greatest, too much social media exposure raises concerns of social exclusion. A new acronym defines that experience: FOMO, short for "fear of missing out." They see the exciting posts of others having a great time, but they are at home feeling isolated and lonely.

The syndrome is not unique to young adults. According to the Pew Research Center, 72 percent of Americans use social media. Previous research has linked social media use to depression, anxiety, impaired sleep, and low self-esteem. However, that earlier research did not determine whether using social media was actually causing these mental symptoms or whether those who were already suffering from mental symptoms were drawn to using social media. More recent research does suggest that using social media causes feelings of depression and loneliness.

Investigators at the University of Pennsylvania randomly assigned 143 students to two study groups: one continued using social media as usual and the other had their social media use significantly restricted (only thirty minutes each day) for three weeks. Those research subjects whose social media use was restricted experienced significantly lower feelings of loneliness and depression compared with the students who had unlimited access. The bottom line is that limiting time on social media to under an hour each day can improve well-being and limit feelings of depression.

TRY THIS

The next time you feel sad or blue, try this easy mindfulness exercise to help you let go of those feelings:

- Sit in a comfortable chair and place your feet flat on the floor, allowing them to point slightly outward.

- Rest your hands on your thighs with your palms facing up and close your eyes.

- Take eight deep, slow breaths in through your nose, and then through your mouth.

- Feel your body relaxing as your mind grows peaceful.

- Continue inhaling and exhaling slowly for another minute or two, then open your eyes.

PSYCHOLOGICAL VERSUS PHYSICAL SYMPTOMS OF DEPRESSION

Most of us think of depression as an emotion, but symptoms of depression and depressive disorders can involve extensive physical components. The first clue that you are feeling depressed could be your chronic back pain flaring up, or you may find yourself waking up in the middle of the night, unable to fall back asleep.

Those physical symptoms of depression are not all in your head. When people get depressed, the body goes through changes. For example, digestion may slow down and lead to abdominal discomfort. Unfortunately, when depressed people have extensive physical symptoms, they may not seek help from mental health professionals, and they may either ignore the symptoms or seek multiple medical evaluations to get to the bottom of their physical complaints.

When someone gets depressed, their brains' neural pathways are changed, affecting the activity in the brains' emotional centers. These centers not only control mood; they also process information that transmits physical sensations, which can contribute to the person's usually uncomfortable physical symptoms.

Chronic stress that leads to symptoms of depression can elevate blood levels with cortisol and other stress hormones. Persistently high cortisol levels can lead to a variety of physical symptoms ranging from difficulty swallowing to muscle aches, shortness of breath, and sweating. Cortisol also increases blood levels of sugar and fats, which are meant to fuel the body so it can take quick action under conditions of acute stress. Unfortunately, when stress and worry drag out or become chronic, the resulting physical changes can suppress and weaken the immune system, leading to infection and illness.

This overlap of physical and psychological symptoms of depression can be confusing to patients and doctors, especially when physical symptoms of depression are mistaken for a medical illness.

Other times, a physical illness may be causing psychological symptoms. Poor concentration or irritability could be due to decreased oxygen to the brain from pneumonia or another infection. And some patients suffer from both depression and physical illness at the same time, which makes it even more challenging to figure out the true underlying source of anxiety symptoms.

PSYCHOLOGICAL AND PHYSICAL SYMPTOMS OF DEPRESSION

Psychological

- Anxiety

- Feelings of guilt

- Hopelessness

- Irritability

- Loneliness

- Loss of interest

- Low self-esteem

- Memory loss

Continued

PSYCHOLOGICAL AND PHYSICAL SYMPTOMS OF DEPRESSION (*CONTINUED*)

- Poor concentration
- Sadness
- Suicidal thoughts
- Worry or rumination

Physical

- Appetite/weight change
- Back pain
- Chest pain
- Digestive problems
- Dizziness
- Dry mouth
- Fatigue
- Headaches
- Insomnia
- Joint pain
- Muscle aches
- Rapid heartbeat, skipped beats

THE DANGERS OF UNTREATED DEPRESSION

Approximately 35 percent of people with depression receive no treatment, and many factors contribute to this unfortunate situation. People suffering from depression tend to focus on their problems and avoid venturing out in the world, which makes them less inclined to seek out help. The limited number of mental health professionals, challenges in accurately diagnosing depression in medical settings, the false assumption that nothing can be done to help, and denial about symptom severity further contribute to undertreatment. Although most people minimize the influence of mental symptoms on their physical health, the scientific evidence is clear that untreated depression can reduce an individual's ability to function in life even more than many other common medical conditions like arthritis, diabetes, and heart disease.

There is no question that shirking professional help for depression can be dangerous to your health and well-being. Untreated depression increases the risk for developing other mental health problems and suicide. As depression-driven physical symptoms and illnesses worsen, the patient's health-care costs will also increase because of inadequate care of physical illnesses, excessive and ineffective use of the health system, and unneeded emergency room visits.

COMMON TYPES OF DEPRESSIVE DISORDERS

- *Situational depression.* Situational depression is also called an adjustment disorder, which is a short-term condition wherein someone has difficulty coping with stressful situations, such as a major life change, loss, or traumatic event. Symptoms may include hopelessness, sadness, frequent crying, nervousness, sleep problems, changes in appetite, and other conditions typical of a depressed state.

- *Major depression.* A persistent feeling of sadness or a lack of interest in outside stimuli accompanied by sleep problems, low energy levels, poor concentration, appetite loss, and other sometimes debilitating symptoms.

- *Bipolar disorder.* Extreme mood swings that include emotional highs (mania or hypomania) and lows (depression). In addition to shifts in mood, patients experience low energy and activity levels and poor concentration and have trouble carrying out daily tasks.

- *Seasonal affective disorder (SAD).* Depression symptoms that usually occur during the fall and winter months when sunlight is limited and improve when the spring season arrives.

- *Dysthymia.* A depressed mood throughout most of the day that occurs on more days than not and has lasted for at least two years.

Depression can be devastating to relationships too. Depressed patients often feel misunderstood and become isolated from family and friends. When severe enough, the illness can devastate the patient's professional life as well. People suffering from depression have difficulty concentrating and feeling motivated to complete work tasks. They tend to log in more sick days and consequently experience significant financial losses.

The good news is that depression can be treated effectively, but the first step toward treatment is for patients to admit that their symptoms are upending their lives. Whether someone has a full-blown depressive disorder or suffers from less profound symptoms, figuring out the type of depression will help determine the most effective treatment for that particular condition.

TREATMENTS FOR DEPRESSION

Regardless of the nature of the depressive symptoms or the type of depressive disorder you or your loved one may be experiencing, effective treatments and self-help strategies are available. The particular intervention that is effective often varies depending on the specific disorder and its severity. For example, patients with major depressive disorder often benefit from both antidepressants and psychotherapy. The

---

DID YOU KNOW?

Stigma about mental illness, limited access to health care, cultural insensitivity, and other factors contribute to racial and ethnic disparities in the diagnosis and treatment of depression. Only 4.2 percent of African Americans are diagnosed with depression, compared with 6.4 percent of white Americans and 7.2 percent of Hispanics. As many as 73 percent of white Americans diagnosed with depression get treated, while only 63 percent of Hispanics and 60 percent of African Americans receive treatment.

---

antidepressants reduce the acute physical and mental symptoms, and the psychotherapy helps patients understand and cope with the psychological and practical challenges of the illness. SAD may respond to these same interventions along with bright-light therapy. Many approaches, such as meditation, physical exercise, and psychotherapy, can be useful for treating nearly all forms of depression.

Psychotherapy. Different forms of talk therapy can reduce symptoms of depression and accelerate remission. By talking with a mental health professional (psychiatrist, psychologist, social worker, or other counselor), patients are better able to understand their behaviors, emotions, and ideas that contribute to their symptoms and then learn how to make positive changes. Cognitive behavioral therapy (CBT) helps people identify and challenge negative patterns of thought about themselves and the world in order to alter their unwanted behavior patterns. Supportive psychotherapy helps people explore troubling issues and provides emotional support.

Medications. Antidepressant medicines, such as Zoloft, Prozac, and other selective serotonin reuptake inhibitors (SSRIs), can reduce the psychological and physical symptoms of depression. Patients with bipolar disorder benefit from antidepressants but also experience mood stabilization from lithium or anticonvulsant medications.

Other interventions. Depressions that are resistant to antidepressant treatments often respond to electroconvulsive therapy (ECT) or may benefit from transcranial magnetic stimulation (TMS), a noninvasive form of brain stimulation.

Lifestyle strategies. Adopting and maintaining healthy behaviors can reduce symptoms of depression. Regular physical exercise and a balanced diet not only improve mood and reduce other symptoms; they also benefit memory and cognitive abilities. Relaxation and mindfulness techniques, such as meditation, hypnosis, yoga, tai chi, and deep breathing, will reduce stress, decrease symptoms of depression, and even rewire neural circuits in the brain.

Your meal choices may impact your risk for depression. People who consume a diet that emphasizes fruits, vegetables, whole grains, fish, olive oil, and low-fat dairy products while minimizing red and/or processed meats, refined grains, sweets, high-fat dairy products, butter, potatoes, and high-fat gravy have a lower risk for developing depression.

Other therapies. Various supplements (e.g., St. John's wort, S-adenosyl methionine [SAM-e]) and innovative treatments (e.g., acupuncture, aromatherapy, biofeedback, meditation, massage therapy) have been used to relieve symptoms of depression. Some of these interventions show promise, are still under scientific investigation, or have not yet been shown to be more effective than placebo.

CHAPTER 2

Do-It-Yourself Strategies for Improving Mood

It is better to light a candle than curse the darkness.
— Terry Pratchett

WHEN WE FEEL DEPRESSED, our natural response is to find a way to relieve the discomfort. It could be as simple as watching a comedy rerun on TV or talking things over with a friend to gain some perspective.

Whether you only experience a low mood from time to time or have a depressive disorder, you've probably tried some do-it-yourself strategies to improve your mood. Perhaps you went to the gym for a workout, tried to meditate, or downloaded a phone app to help you elevate your mood. These well-known approaches often help, but there are other strategies that may reduce your symptoms even more.

A lot of us feel depressed because we take on too many tasks. Becoming overcommitted is easy, while learning to delegate can be harder. Most people don't know that simply *asking* others for assistance can make them feel empowered and lift their mood tremendously.

TRY THIS

Make a list of your various appointments and to-do items coming up in the next week. Prioritize your list according to what you absolutely must do yourself, what you can ask others to do, and what you can put off until a later time. This simple exercise can free you up to take care of other things you have put on the back burner and help you feel less overwhelmed.

Various forms of therapy can help people gain a better perspective on their feelings, but a good conversation with an empathic friend can also be very effective in reducing stress. If you are candid with your friend about what's bothering you, you may experience relief by venting some of your concerns, and your friend may be able to offer a different perspective.

Learning to recognize what triggers your negative feelings is critical when considering ways to dissipate your mood symptoms. For example, if you know that a certain person always seems to bring you down, try distancing yourself from that individual and minimizing future contact unless it's absolutely necessary.

Kent never liked visiting his older sister, Cindy. She always seemed to be in a bad mood, and after his visits, he felt sad too. Sure, Cindy had been having a tough time with her job and her marriage, but Kent thought that she contributed to those problems. Unfortunately, he never spoke up and talked with her about his perspective because he thought it would upset her even more and lead to an argument.

He felt guilty when he cut back on his visits to his sister, so Kent decided to find other ways to avoid getting so upset when he was with her. While searching the internet for self-help methods, he saw that many people got relief from meditation. He had practiced meditation during college, so he decided to give it another try. Right before and after each visit with his sister, he spent ten minutes meditating. He found that Cindy didn't upset him as much thanks to his meditations. After a few weeks of feeling better about their relationship, Kent introduced his sister to meditation. Cindy found it helpful too, and the two of them started meditating together when he visited.

Once a depression trigger is identified, it becomes easier to address. Below is a list of common triggers and some do-it-yourself remedies. See if any apply to you so you can begin to devise your own ways to lessen the strength of your depression triggers.

DEPRESSION-PROMOTING TRIGGERS AND WHAT YOU CAN DO ABOUT THEM

Trigger

- Too much social media

- Binge eating

- Isolation and loneliness

- Being too sedentary

Solution

- Only use social media for a specific purpose and avoid logging on just for something to do

- Rid the house of unhealthy snacks and keep healthy foods accessible

- Try to meet new people and reach out to old friends

- Establish a regular time each day to exercise and then stick to it

Depression, like any negative emotion, can be infectious. If you spend time with depressed people, those feelings may eventually ooze into your psyche. Making an effort to keep a positive outlook is another helpful strategy for improving your mood and the moods of those around you. Learning optimism is not as hard as it may seem. Some people are born seeing the cup half full. They appreciate the good things in their lives and avoid dwelling on the bad.

TRY THIS

- Think of a situation that makes you depressed–perhaps a disagreement with a friend or worrying over your health issues.

- In your mind, play out your anticipated negative outcome of this situation, such as possibly losing that friendship, getting severely ill, and so on.

- Begin to concentrate on your breathing. Take a few deep, slow inhales and exhales. Continue to focus on your breath coming in and going out and feel yourself relaxing mentally and physically.

- Consider the current depression-provoking situation and try to see the bigger picture: even if you lose this friendship, job, or opportunity, you still have many other important people in your life, and more opportunities await. Try to remind yourself of how well you have been caring for your needs and how much you have accomplished over the years.

Using this approach allows you to step back, relax, and put your concerns into perspective so you can recover a positive attitude more quickly.

The following self-help approaches have all been found to help reduce stress and shift people's moods in a positive direction. The best way to discover which method or methods work best for you is to try them out.

RELAXATION TECHNIQUES

Stress and anxiety often trigger symptoms of depression, so strategies that help people experience a relaxation response can help improve their mood. Although systematic controlled studies of these strategies do not always demonstrate an effect, many people report that they do experience an improvement in their mood symptoms. The following are some relaxation techniques that have the potential to lessen feelings of depression or anxiety or both.

Progressive Muscle Relaxation

The anxiety symptoms that often accompany depression may lead to taut muscles that can cause chronic aches and pains, and progressive muscle relaxation may help relieve such symptoms. This exercise involves gradually scanning the body from top to bottom and systematically releasing muscular tension along the way.

TRY THIS

- Sit in a comfortable chair or on a mat.

- Breathe slowly and deeply throughout the exercise with your eyes closed.

- Pay attention to any tension in your scalp and forehead and consciously make an effort to relax those muscles.

- After a moment, focus your attention on the muscles around your eyes and release any tension there. Then focus on letting those relaxed feelings spread down to your jaw, neck, and shoulders.

- Continue to relax every muscle group in your body as you move down to your arms, torso, buttocks, and so on until you reach your toes.

- Once you have completely scanned your entire body, take a last deep inhale and exhale, then open your eyes.

Meditation

To get started, make yourself comfortable in either a sitting or lying position and focus your attention on a phrase, breath, sound, or object. Most people find that their mind soon wanders. However, after a while, they are able to recognize when this mind-wandering happens and gently guide their attention back to their breathing, mantra, or whatever else they have chosen to focus on.

Meditation has been shown to improve mood and memory while altering brain neural circuits. Many studies have demonstrated that meditation increases the size of gray matter, the brain's outer rim where neurons reside. Meditation also increases overall brain-wave function and activates the thinking brain (frontal lobe) and emotional brain (amygdala).

QUICK MEDITATION BREAK

Take a few minutes to try this mindfulness exercise:

- Sit in a comfortable chair and place your feet flat on the floor, allowing them to point slightly outward.

- Rest your hands gently on your thighs with your palms facing up and close your eyes.

- Begin taking slow breaths in and out through your nose. Focus on the coolness of the air as it enters your nostrils and the warmth of the air as you slowly exhale.

- If your mind wanders to random thoughts about errands you have to do, calls you have to make, and so on, gently guide it back to the feeling in your nostrils as the air moves in and out.

- Experience your body relax as your mind grows peaceful.

- Continue for another minute or two, then open your eyes.

MEDITATION TECHNIQUES

- *Guided meditation.* In this form of meditation, an instructor serves as a guide and makes suggestions about what to focus attention on (e.g., images, sounds, breathing). This is a helpful way for beginners to get started, and you can download guided meditation apps on your smartphone or tablet.

- *Affirmative meditation.* This form of meditation uses positive affirmations about health, mood, confidence, or other areas in order to encourage positive feelings and thoughts.

- *Mindfulness meditation.* This approach focuses on becoming aware of and staying in the present from moment to moment. It becomes effective when the meditator learns to accept any mind-wandering without becoming judgmental.

- *Transcendental meditation.* This method trains the mind to become calm, silent, and "empty" and involves repeating a mantra, word, or phrase.

- *Progressive muscle relaxation.* These exercises involve monitoring tension in a particular muscle or body area, relaxing that region, and then progressively spreading that relaxation throughout the body.

- *Self-hypnosis.* The practitioner becomes relaxed while focusing attention on particular aspects of thinking, believing, or perception, often in order to control habits and behaviors or to reduce pain.

A popular variety of meditation involves achieving mindfulness, a mental state characterized by self-regulation of attention toward present-moment experiences accompanied by an accepting, non-judgmental perspective toward the experience. A meta-analysis of randomized controlled trials demonstrated the benefits of mindfulness-based interventions for people who are depressed.

Many forms of meditation offer these types of beneficial effects. When starting out, it can be helpful to try out various styles to see which one works best for you.

Autogenic Training

Autogenic training is a simple mental exercise for retraining the mind in order to lower stress levels and calm the body. The person makes mental or verbal commands to control their heartbeat, breathing, temperature, blood pressure, pain, and more. Autogenic training is similar to biofeedback in that they both focus on the autonomic nervous system, which regulates body functions that normally are not controlled by the conscious mind. The biofeedback method requires the use of an electric biofeedback device to objectively monitor and provide feedback on certain physical functions, but it is not necessary for autogenic training.

Journaling

Keeping a diary or journal can help people with low moods gain perspective and reduce negative thinking. Maintaining a log or diary of activities and emotional reactions over time allows people to reflect on their experiences and feelings in order to gain insight into them. Simply writing about feelings, just as with talking about them, can in itself reduce stress levels.

If you have never kept a journal, you might start by finding a quiet and comfortable place where you won't be interrupted. Begin writing about whatever comes to mind and remember that spelling and grammar don't count. You just need to enter a date and reflect on your thoughts and feelings in the moment.

RESTFUL SLEEP

Disrupted sleep is often a symptom of depression. Insomnia can take the form of trouble falling asleep, trouble staying asleep, waking up too early, or getting up and not feeling refreshed. When depressed people remain awake in the middle of the night, they often ruminate and focus on negative thoughts and emotions, which can make them feel even worse.

Insomnia has been shown to increase the risk for developing depression. Sleep problems can also worsen physical illnesses such as hypertension, diabetes, and obesity, which can further threaten brain health and increase the risk for cognitive decline and depressed mood.

Fortunately, self-help methods can reduce symptoms of insomnia and improve sleep. Many people will use meditation, deep-breathing exercises, and progressive muscle relaxation to help them get to sleep at night and fall back asleep if they wake up too early.

It is helpful to keep in mind that heart problems, other physical illnesses, and medication side effects can disrupt sleep. If you think you have a problem sleeping or your sleep patterns have changed for no reason, discuss your concerns with your doctor to find out if there is an underlying medical cause.

Cognitive behavior therapy (CBT) for insomnia, a type of talk therapy, has been shown to improve sleep patterns by teaching people to identify and alter the behaviors that disrupt their sleep. You can learn this technique for yourself by using one of several online CBT programs for insomnia (e.g., SHUTi, Sleepio).

Depending on the cause of your sleep problem, your doctor may or may not prescribe a medication. Depressed patients may sleep better when they take a sedating antidepressant medicine, but sleeping pills like Ambien or Lunesta can become habit forming. Also, some over-the-counter sleep aids have been shown to have memory side effects, especially for older adults who are already becoming forgetful. It's always best to try self-help methods to improve sleep to avoid the side effects and dependency that many people experience from sedatives.

PHYSICAL EXERCISE

Numerous studies have shown that aerobic conditioning improves memory, mood, and energy levels. It also reduces brain-damaging neural inflammation and increases mental focus.

Most experts recommend daily exercise, which can take the form of brisk walks, jogging, swimming, or sports, and it is not necessary to engage in extensive exercise to reap mind-health benefits. Investigators at the Harvard T. H. Chan School of Public Health found that fifteen minutes of running or one hour of walking each day can reduce the risk of developing major depression by 26 percent.

Many people prefer fitness classes or competitive sports to get their exercise, while others like to work out on their own. When you do exercise with others, you reap further benefits from the social interaction that can lift your mood. You'll have a better chance of sticking with your exercise regimen if you find one that is enjoyable and convenient. When beginning any new exercise program, start low and go slow to avoid injury and gradually build stamina.

Another great mood-enhancing option is yoga, which involves specific postures, breathing, and

STRATEGIES FOR GETTING A GOOD NIGHT'S SLEEP

- Avoid daytime naps so you will feel tired at bedtime.

- Pick a regular bedtime and stick to it.

- Try not to eat, use the computer, watch TV, or talk on the phone while lying in bed before going to sleep. These activities may hype you up and make it harder to fall asleep.

- Avoid consuming caffeine or drinking a lot of liquids in the evening.

- Engage in exercise every day so you feel sleepier at night.

- Listen to calming music and use a timer to shut it off automatically.

- Meditate to help you fall asleep.

- Try this systematic strategy that promotes better sleep habits:
  - Get into bed at the same time each evening.
  - Meditate or use another relaxation method to settle down.
  - If you are not asleep in twenty minutes, get out of bed and do something else–read a book, listen to music, and so on.
  - When you begin feeling tired, go back to bed and try to fall asleep.

- If you're still awake after twenty minutes, get out of bed and do something else again.
- Keep repeating this routine throughout the night.
- Make sure you don't nap the next day, and repeat the previous steps the next night.
- By the third night, it should be easier for you to fall asleep on your first attempt.

meditative elements. The slow, deliberate meditative postures and movements of tai chi have also been shown to improve mood, memory, and physical stamina while altering brain neural circuitry for the better.

Many people love to dance, which is an excellent way to combine an aerobic workout with mood-boosting social interactions and the cognitive challenge of keeping track of your movements and steps. Brain scans of experienced dancers demonstrate strengthened neural circuits in regions involved in motor control, balance, and social interactions compared to scans of beginners.

Catching up on household chores is yet another way to get a pretty good workout. Raking leaves and making beds for just thirty minutes can burn off 100 or more calories. Of course, the particular chore will determine the number of calories burned. For the average 155-pound individual, thirty minutes of cooking will burn about 100 calories, while the same amount of time gardening or mowing the lawn can knock off about 170 calories.

Another way to get some mood-boosting exercise is to go shopping at the mall. Walking briskly between stores gives you an aerobic workout, and you'll also benefit from the neural stimulation that comes from searching through items for the right sizes and colors. If you shop with a friend, you'll enjoy additional brain-health benefits from the social interaction, which may reduce stress levels, stimulate your neural circuits, and make exercising more fun (as long as you don't run up too large of a credit card bill).

DID YOU KNOW?

- Cardiovascular conditioning releases feel-good endorphins and other natural brain chemicals that can lift mood almost immediately.

- For most people, genetic inheritance contributes less to their risk for depression than nongenetic factors. Studies of identical twins, who share the exact same genes, show that there's only a 30 percent chance that both will develop depression.

Most of the research on the mood benefits of exercise has focused on aerobic conditioning; however, strength training offers additional benefits. Both forms of physical exercise promote cardiac health, which improves the efficiency of our hearts in pumping oxygen and nutrients into our brain cells, which in turn boosts physical and mental energy while stabilizing mood. If you're pressed for time, try interval training, which involves periods of intense exertion alternated with periods of rest or lighter exercise. Recent research indicates that you can receive the same health benefits from this pattern of exercise in one-fourth of the time needed for endurance training.

PHYSICAL ACTIVITIES THAT IMPROVE MOOD

- *Cardiovascular conditioning:* climbing, cycling, elliptical, interval training, jogging, running, swimming, treadmill, walking, yoga

- *Competitive sports:* badminton, baseball, football, ping-pong, basketball, racquetball, soccer, tennis

- *Dancing:* ballroom, tap, disco, hip hop

- *Strength training:* free weights, Pilates, resistance bands, yoga, weight-lifting machines

- *Other activities:* shopping, gardening, household chores

NUTRITION FOR A BETTER MOOD

Most people know that making good food choices can fortify their physical health, but a less appreciated fact about eating well is that it can also strengthen mind health. The way people eat can also impact their mood state. Dining alone can feel isolating and even depressing, but when we share meals with others, we are able to enjoy the social interaction, which reduces stress and improves overall well-being.

Fruits, whole grains, and vegetables provide essential vitamins and minerals that can lower a person's risk for depression. Moreover, consuming foods that are rich in omega-3 fats like fish and nuts is associated with a better mood state. Certain carbohydrates, when consumed in moderation, have a calming effect, perhaps because they raise levels of serotonin, a mood-enhancing brain messenger. Experts speculate that low levels of serotonin in the brain may be linked to "carb cravings," which trigger the impulse to pounce on the bread basket at meals. Some protein-rich foods like chicken, turkey, and tuna contain the amino acid tryptophan, which can increase serotonin in the brain.

Most people experience mood improvements when they consume so-called comfort foods, such as grilled cheese sandwiches, macaroni and cheese, or a bowl of sugary cereal. Unfortunately, such comfort foods usually offer only temporary mood boosts and, when consumed in excess, can lead to health problems associated with being overweight or obese, not to mention the guilt many people feel after a comfort-food binge.

Regular consumption of fast foods, processed foods, and sweets generally worsen mood compared with eating natural foods like poultry, seeds, and nuts. One type of diet that promotes both heart and brain health is the Mediterranean-style diet, which emphasizes fruits, vegetables, lean proteins, and omega-3 fats from fish, nuts, or flax seed. This diet's nutritional value results in part from its anti-inflammatory properties, which protect our brains and bodies from the daily wear and tear of oxidative stress caused by inflammation. In addition to improving mood, it supports memory and cognitive health. Research indicates that limiting the intake of refined sugars and processed foods will reduce brain-damaging inflammation.

A brain-healthy diet includes whole grains, which are complex carbohydrates that take longer to digest, helping stabilize blood-sugar levels and provide a steady supply of serotonin to the brain. Such carbs are said to be low on the glycemic index (GI). The GI ranks carbohydrates from zero to one hundred depending on their complexity and how rapidly they are digested and absorbed as sugar (glucose) into the blood. For better mood and brain health, it's best to substitute healthy low-GI carbs for high-GI

carbs because the latter will spike blood-sugar levels and lead to subsequent blood-sugar dives. Such
dips in blood-sugar levels can trigger hypoglycemia,
a potentially serious mental and physical state that
worsens mood and causes sweating, dizziness, and a
pounding or racing heart.

Examples of high-GI foods include baked potatoes, dried dates, white baguettes, instant mashed
potatoes, instant rice, bagels, Cheerios, Cocoa Puffs,
cornflakes, French fries, jelly beans, pretzels, puffed-
wheat cereal, rice cakes, and soda crackers. Of course,
occasionally consuming some of these foods in moderation won't throw you into major depression. However, nutritional experts recommend substituting
such low-GI foods as apples, apricots, bean sprouts,
cashews, fettuccine, grapefruit, lentils, lima beans,
nonfat yogurt, peanuts, prunes, skim milk, soy-
beans, or wheat tortillas.

Most people drink caffeinated beverages, such as
tea or coffee, which usually leads to an immediate
boost in energy and mood. However, too much caffeine can cause anxiety followed by low mood levels
once the caffeine wears off. Caffeine consumption
has been associated with a lower risk for developing dementia or Parkinson's disease, but only if consumed in moderation, which translates to one to two
cups of coffee each day.

TECHNOLOGY USE CAN AFFECT YOUR MOOD

Thanks to remarkable innovations in technology, we get instantaneous gratification from our many devices. They provide access to vast amounts of information and offer the ability to connect with family, friends, and colleagues almost anywhere in the world. Our computers, tablets, and smartphones are able to enhance our personal lives, streamline our work, free up our time, and help us communicate quickly and efficiently. While such benefits may reduce stress and enhance mood, too much technology can make people feel anxious and depressed.

Social media platforms like Facebook, Instagram, and Snapchat allow us to remain in touch with each other and share our thoughts, feelings, videos, and photographs throughout the day (and night), but such platforms leave some people feeling sad about their own, less exciting lives and even increase their emotional isolation. Such isolation may bring on feelings of loneliness and self-doubt, which can contribute to a depressed mood. I often recommend that people pick and choose their technology tools wisely in order to help reduce their stress levels rather than increase them.

Many websites and apps have been designed to help people who suffer from mood problems, and the Anxiety and Depression Association of America (ADAA) as well as other organizations provide reviews of many of them (see box). These programs vary in their ease of use, how much they can be personalized for the individual user, the research evidence backing up their effectiveness, and the availability of interactive features. Several of the apps can be helpful for people to use on their own as well as in conjunction with traditional therapy.

CBT is a form of talk therapy that helps people develop coping skills by learning to change their thinking, feelings, and behavior. Studies of internet-based versions of CBT for depression suggest that a relatively greater depression severity; being separated, widowed, or divorced; having a higher level of education; and being a woman can predict greater depressive-symptom improvement from internet-based CBT.

STAYING CONNECTED WITH FRIENDS AND FAMILY

When we spend time with people we care about, it often takes our focus away from ourselves, lifts our mood, and allows us to feel connected. It's even better when we combine social interactions with other mood-boosting strategies like meditation, exercise, and healthy nutrition. Sharing an exhilarating walk with an empathic companion not only provides stress-reducing exercise; it allows us to discuss and sort out the problems that may be bringing us down.

APPS FOR IMPROVING MOOD

- *Breathe2Relax:* teaches breathing techniques to help with stress management

- *Happify:* increases positive emotions through exercises and games that are supported by positive psychology and mindfulness research

- *Headspace:* provides meditation techniques to improve mood

- *iCBT app:* assists users in identifying, appraising, and reappraising negative thoughts and cognitive distortions

- *MoodKit:* teaches general CBT concepts and helps with self-monitoring

- *MoodTools:* targets depression and offers education on risk factors and treatment approaches, a depression-symptom questionnaire (PHQ-9), a thought diary, a suicide safety plan, and meditation guides

- *Pacifica:* offers deep-breathing and positive-thinking techniques

- *T2 Mood Tracker:* tracks emotional states over time

Enjoying a healthy meal with a friend, taking a group meditation class, or having a conversation with a close relative or pal will tend to reduce feelings of sadness or loneliness.

Support groups can also be helpful in dealing with depression or sadness. When we share our feelings and learn about how others cope, it can offer insights into how to better manage our own emotional challenges. The ADAA provides resources for finding local and online support groups for people experiencing various kinds of depression.

Taking medications or receiving medical treatment for depression does not preclude using self-help approaches. In fact, many people find that combining do-it-yourself strategies with conventional treatments for depression can be the most effective way to relieve symptoms, recover more rapidly, and remain in remission.

Whether or not you are practicing self-help strategies, if feelings of depression are disrupting your everyday life, it is important to consider seeking professional help. Even if you're not sure if you need it, it's best to err on the conservative side and seek help. Many effective treatments are available for depressive disorders, and untreated depression can result in serious consequences.

CHAPTER 3

Conventional Depression Treatments That Work

*I told my psychiatrist that everyone
hates me. He said I was being
ridiculous—everyone hasn't met
me yet.*

               —Rodney Dangerfield

IF YOU FIND THAT your feelings of sadness are disrupting your everyday life, then you may well be suffering from a depressive disorder. The good news is that effective conventional treatments are available, and most patients with depressive disorders are able to recover.

* * * * *

Several years ago, I received a call from a friend about his sixty-one-year-old wife, Charlotte, who thought she was having a nervous breakdown. For the past week, she didn't have the energy to go to work, wasn't sleeping well, had trouble getting out of bed in the morning, cried often throughout the day, and said that her life felt unbearable.

I told him that if Charlotte was expressing any thoughts of suicide, she needed to go to the emergency room. I offered to make a call about getting her a bed, and I said I'd meet them there to smooth the way. My friend said Charlotte wasn't so bad that she needed to go to the psych ward, and besides, he didn't want her to be labeled as having a mental illness.

I agreed to speak to her but was concerned about her husband's denial of the seriousness of her condition. Many people suffering from mental illness and their families are too ashamed to ask for the help they need, which is unfortunate because common mental conditions like depression—the leading cause of suicide—have effective treatments. Charlotte's sadness, social withdrawal, sleep deprivation, and other symptoms pointed to a severe depression that required attention.

On the phone, I encouraged her to come in, but Charlotte refused. She was convinced that there was nothing that could help, and she was determined to get through this on her own. Fortunately, it didn't sound like she was suicidal, so I gave her my cell phone number and told her to call me anytime.

Charlotte was not alone in her unwarranted pessimism about treatments for mental illness. Many people still believe that medicines are overused and that talk therapies are ineffective, and some are simply afraid of facing their own psychological issues. Untreated depression, however, increases the risk for drug or alcohol addiction, disrupts relationships, causes problems at work, worsens physical health, and can lead to suicidal behavior. A recent study showed that two-thirds of depressed older adults are not receiving treatments to alleviate their symptoms.

Charlotte called me back the next day and opened up to me about her symptoms, which were consistent with major depression. I explained that such episodes do improve with proper treatment, and her prognosis was quite good. I said that because she was not suicidal, she didn't have to come into the hospital. I arranged for her to see another geriatric psychiatrist with experience in treating patients who are reluctant to get help. Charlotte's husband called me about two weeks later to thank me: he already saw tremendous improvement from her outpatient psychotherapy and antidepressant treatment.

I have treated many patients like Charlotte who respond quite well to conventional treatments for depression, such as antidepressant medicine, psychotherapy, or both. Exactly which treatment makes sense depends on the particular type of depressive disorder. Of course, the severity of symptoms, whether family members and friends are available for support, and the patient's own motivation to get help will impact the treatment outcome.

Very often, mental health professionals will use a combination of approaches that are in part determined by the clinician's training and area of expertise. For medication treatment, often a psychiatrist who has a medical degree will prescribe the medicine, although many internists and family doctors are comfortable treating depression with medications as well. Many psychiatrists also offer talk therapies; however, psychologists, marriage and family counselors, and other mental health professionals are able to provide psychotherapy treatments too.

FINDING THE RIGHT MENTAL HEALTH PROFESSIONAL

Whether you require medication, psychotherapy, or both, it's important that patients form a collaborative relationship with their clinician. Feeling comfortable communicating with your doctor without feeling judged or dismissed will increase the likelihood that you will trust that clinician and remain in treatment long enough to get better. Many patients first inform their primary care doctor about their depression symptoms, and family physicians and internists are able to prescribe antidepressants. However, a psychiatrist, psychologist, or other mental health practitioner with training and experience in mood disorders can be even more helpful in the assessment, diagnosis, and treatment of the condition. If patients find that they are not improving while being treated by their family doctor, it's important to seek out a second opinion, perhaps from a behavioral health specialist, to determine next steps.

Many people do well with therapists recommended by a trusted friend or physician. Regardless of the referral source, I recommend that for the first visit, patients bring in a list of specific questions that they wish to ask. Keeping a journal that details your symptoms and what triggers them will also help you and your mental health practitioner or doctor understand your mood problems better.

Before beginning a medication for depression, make sure that the prescribing doctor is aware of all other medications or over-the-counter drugs or supplements you are taking. Medicines and supplements can interact to increase side effects; if you do experience side effects, consult with your doctor as soon as possible to determine whether you should stop taking the medication. Your doctor may wish to taper down the dose rather than stop the drug suddenly. Adhering to the doctor's recommended dose will ensure that your medicines will have their greatest effect and minimize the risk of side effects.

MEDICINES FOR TREATING DEPRESSION

Several different types of medicines have been shown to be effective for a variety of depressive disorders. While antidepressant drugs (e.g., Zoloft, Prozac) are the mainstay of treatment, other medicines can be helpful as well. If a patient suffers from bipolar disorder, lithium or an anticonvulsant medicine (e.g., Depakote, Lamictal) may be used to stabilize mood. Patients with accompanying anxiety may receive a benzodiazepine (e.g., Valium, Xanax) or buspirone (Buspar).

My strategy for prescribing any of these medicines is to begin with the lowest dosage. After starting low, I go slow when increasing the dosage level in order to minimize any potential side effects as I determine the optimal therapeutic dose for a particular patient. This strategy is particularly important when treating older adults who tend to be sensitive to even small doses of medicines. The other advantage to this dosing strategy is that people who do develop mild side effects are often better able to adjust to them after a few weeks.

Antidepressants

These medicines are effective in lifting depression by increasing the levels of serotonin, norepinephrine, and other neurotransmitters or brain messengers that control mood states. It's important to inform patients and their families that it may take a few weeks to notice any mood effects, and sometimes others are more aware of mood improvements before the patient notices them. When people are not aware of this typical delay in treatment response, they are more likely to get discouraged and stop taking their medicine too soon, before they experience any benefits.

In the past, tricyclic antidepressants were often the first-line treatments for depression, but newer medicines with fewer side effects, such as selective serotonin reuptake inhibitors (SSRIs), serotonin/norepinephrine reuptake inhibitors (SNRIs), and noradrenergic/specific serotonergic antidepressants (NaSSAs) are usually used. Other medicines that have been shown to be effective are monoamine oxidase inhibitors (MAOIs) and the serotonin antagonist and reuptake inhibitor (SARI) trazodone. When a medication is found to be effective in treating the symptoms, the patient may continue taking it for months or even years.

Adverse effects may emerge with any of these medications; however, some "side effects" can actually help patients with their symptoms. For example, a patient with major depression and insomnia may do well when a sedating antidepressant such as Desyrel or Remeron is taken at bedtime.

ANTIDEPRESSANT MEDICATIONS

Category	Examples	Possible Side Effects
SSRI	Celexa (citalopram), Lexapro (escitalopram), Paxil (paroxetine), Prozac (fluoxetine), Zoloft (sertraline)	Nausea, upset stomach, weight gain, decreased libido, drowsiness
SNRI	Cymbalta (duloxetine hydrochloride), Effexor (venlafaxine), Pristiq (desvenlafaxine)	Nausea, insomnia, dizziness, drowsiness, weight loss, headaches
NaSSA	Remeron (mirtazapine)	Weight gain, drowsiness
Tricyclics	Anafranil (clomipramine), Elavil (amitriptyline), Norpramin (desipramine), Pamelor (nortiptyline)	Dry mouth, constipation, sweating, urinary retention, slowed heartbeat
MAOI	Nardil (phenelzine), Parnate (tranylcypromine)	Dizziness (when standing up), dry mouth, constipation, dangerous interaction with certain foods/drugs

SARI	Desyrel (trazodone)	Nausea, vomiting, diarrhea, drowsiness, dizziness, fatigue, blurred vision, headaches, muscle aches, dry mouth, stuffy nose, constipation, decreased libido

Benzodiazepines

These medicines are usually used to treat acute anxiety, since they calm the nervous system almost immediately. When combined with antidepressants, benzodiazepines have been found to decrease symptoms of depression during the first month of treatment compared with using antidepressants alone. After that first month, however, the combination treatment has no advantage and heightens the risk of side effects. Doctors are thus reluctant to use benzodiazepines in treating depression, particularly over a long time period.

Older benzodiazepines like Valium (diazepam), Klonopin (clonazepam), and Librium (chlordiazepoxide) are long-acting medicines, and their levels build up over time, which leads to more side effects. Newer, safer, and shorter-acting drugs like Xanax (alprazolam) and Ativan (lorazepam) accumulate less in the body, lowering some of the risks for adverse effects. These drugs should not be taken with alcohol or other sedatives and should be avoided when driving an automobile, since their use is linked to higher rates of car accidents. Another issue with benzodiazepines is that people can become dependent on them over time.

Buspirone

Buspirone (Buspar) has been shown to be effective in treating symptoms of generalized anxiety disorder, but it has also been used for depression, either alone or along with an antidepressant medication. It can take several weeks before patients notice benefits, and it does not cause dependence.

Lithium

Lithium is an element that is used primarily to treat bipolar disorder. It increases the activity of chemical messengers in the brain and helps stabilize the patient's mood relatively quickly. When patients take lithium, it is important for the doctor to check blood levels to help avoid side effects, which can include nausea, diarrhea, dizziness, heart-rhythm changes, muscle weakness, and fatigue. Often the side effects diminish with continued use, but some side effects may persist, such as fine tremors (i.e., involuntary quivering movements), frequent urination, and thirst. Other possible side effects include acne, rashes, and thyroid problems.

The body eliminates lithium through the kidneys, so people with kidney disease need to take lower doses. It also increases a brain chemical called serotonin, so patients taking SSRIs and other antidepressants that increase serotonin need to be cautious of drug interactions. Patients also need to be careful about possible interactions with antihypertensive medicines, anticonvulsants, muscle relaxants, and anti-inflammatory drugs.

Anticonvulsants

These medications are used for treating seizures and epilepsy, but they also are effective as mood stabilizers, particularly for patients with bipolar disorder. They are often prescribed to control mania and are used alone, with lithium, or with an antipsychotic drug. Examples include Depakote (divalproex sodium), Lamictal (lamotrigine), and Tegretol (carbamazepine). Dizziness, fatigue, nausea, tremors, rashes, and weight gain are common side effects.

Atypical Antipsychotics

Antipsychotic medicines were developed to treat people who are out of touch with reality because of hallucinations (false sensory perceptions) or delusions (false fixed beliefs). In recent years, a second

generation of these medicines called atypical antipsychotics have replaced the older ones (e.g., Thorazine,
Haldol). Examples include Seroquel (quetiapine),
Zyprexa (olanzapine), Risperdal (risperidone), Abilify (aripiprazole), and Geodon (ziprasidone). Possible side effects include dry mouth, blurred vision,
dizziness, weakness, restlessness, movement abnormalities, stiffness, and weight gain. Antipsychotics
can occasionally cause akathisia, a sense of restlessness and need to move. Long-term use may lead to
tardive dyskinesia, which is repetitive, involuntary
movements of the face and body.

Ketamine

In recent years, this anesthetic drug has been used
off-label (i.e., not approved by the FDA) for severe or
refractory depression. When administered as a slow
intravenous infusion in very low doses, its antidepressant effects are rapid and observed within hours.
However, the benefits are lost after several days or up
to two weeks following administration. Side effects
include dream-like feelings, blurred or double vision,
jerky muscle movements, dizziness, drowsiness, nausea, vomiting, loss of appetite, and insomnia. Some
psychiatric investigators think that the drug holds
promise for treating refractory depression.

MEDICINES USED TO TREAT DEPRESSION AND ASSOCIATED SYMPTOMS

- Antidepressants

- Benzodiazepines

- Buspirone

- Lithium

- Anticonvulsants

- Atypical antipsychotics

- Ketamine

OTHER MEDICAL TREATMENTS FOR DEPRESSION

Electroconvulsive Therapy

Electroconvulsive therapy (ECT) is another treatment for depression that often works when other treatments have failed. It involves administering to an anesthetized patient small electric currents into the brain, which deliberately triggers a brief seizure. It is generally safe and can provide swift and considerable improvements in severe depression, psychotic depression, and treatment-resistant depression.

Many ECT patients notice symptom improvement after approximately six sessions over a period of two weeks, whereas antidepressant medicines can take longer to be effective, sometimes even months. Some people may experience temporary side effects from ECT including confusion and memory loss, and the number of treatments needed depends on the severity of symptoms and how quickly patients show improvement.

Neuromodulation Therapies

An estimated 10 to 30 percent of patients with major depression do not improve from conventional treatments or only show a partial response. Several neuromodulation options are available for these treatment-resistant patients. Neuromodulation is defined as methods that alter nerve activity through the targeted delivery of a stimulus to specific sites in the body in order to normalize the function of nervous tissue. Some techniques are invasive and involve implanting stimulation devices in the brain, while others are noninvasive. Recently, clinicians and investigators have focused on three particular interventions: transcranial magnetic stimulation (TMS), deep brain stimulation, and trigeminal nerve stimulation.

TMS is a noninvasive procedure for treating depressions that are resistant to other treatments. The procedure has been FDA approved since 2008 for major depression and involves painlessly deliver-ing repetitive magnetic pulses to stimulate particular nerve cells in brain regions that control mood and depression. Unlike ECT, TMS does not cause seizures and no anesthesia is needed.

TMS is usually performed in a doctor's office, and sessions are normally done five days a week for four to six weeks. Although it is usually well tolerated and effective, TMS can cause some mild to moderate short-term side effects including lightheadedness, headaches, and tingling or twitching of facial muscles. Rare and more severe side effects may include hearing loss, mania, and seizures. When TMS is successful, depression symptoms improve and often go away altogether.

Deep brain stimulation involves surgically implanting a device in the brain that delivers small electric shocks. It is used to reduce tremors and block involuntary movements in patients with movement disorders. It is currently under study for the treatment of depression. Another neuromodulation method under investigation for depression is called trigeminal nerve stimulation, which involves sending mild electrical signals that stimulate the trigeminal nerve, the largest cranial nerve, in order to alter the activity of targeted brain regions.

Psilocybin with Psychological Support

Psilocybin, a naturally occurring plant alkaloid, is currently under study for treatment-resistant depression. It has been showing promise when patients receive two very small oral doses (ten and twenty-five milligrams) one week apart along with supportive psychotherapy. The intervention appears to be well tolerated and improves symptoms after five weeks.

PSYCHOTHERAPY

Several forms of psychotherapy (or talk therapy) have been used in the treatment of depression. A variety of licensed mental health practitioners are available for these treatments, including marriage and family counselors, psychologists, nurse practitioners, and psychiatrists. Each therapist tends to focus on the form of therapy they have training in, ranging from cognitive behavioral therapy (CBT) to psychodynamic or insight-oriented approaches.

For depression, several of these forms of therapy are considered evidence-based, which means that systematic studies have shown that they have demonstrated effectiveness. The type of psychotherapy that will be best for each individual will depend on the form and severity of the depression as well as the patient's personality and particular preferences. Many psychotherapists are able to incorporate a combination of several different approaches, and some psychiatrists use medication treatments for depression along with psychotherapy. Regardless of the form of therapy, it is essential that the therapist

FINDING A THERAPIST

The National Institute of Mental Health (NIMH) provides resources to help people find an appropriate therapist in their area. Below are examples of both professional and national advocacy organizations that list directories of professionals. You can easily find them online.

- Academy of Cognitive Therapy

- Association for Behavioral Therapies

- American Academy of Child & Adolescent Psychiatry

- American Association for Geriatric Psychiatry

- American Psychiatric Association

- American Psychological Association

- Anxiety and Depression Association of America

- National Association of Social Workers

- Society of Clinical Psychology

- Mental Health America

- National Alliance on Mental Illness

has a certain level of empathy so that the patient's emotional point of view can be considered with sensitivity.

When choosing a therapist, it's important to review the clinician's credentials and experience before getting started and then discuss your goals for the psychotherapy. Keep in mind that whatever you discuss with your therapist is always considered confidential except in cases of medical emergencies or when there is imminent danger to the patient or others.

Although depressed patients often receive psychotherapy in conjunction with antidepressant medications, many types of talk therapy are performed on their own and can provide psychological perspectives and specific cognitive tools to help reduce symptoms.

Cognitive Behavioral Therapy (CBT)

With CBT, patients identify thoughts, feelings, and behaviors that are linked to their depressive symptoms. For some patients with mild or moderate depression, the therapy can be as effective as or better than antidepressant medication.

The cognitive therapy component of CBT helps patients recognize and alter the distorted thoughts and beliefs that influence their behaviors and contribute to their depressive symptoms. Once patients have identified their distorted thinking and its resulting behaviors, the therapist can help them examine and better understand how their negative thinking impacts their lives. As a result, the patient learns and adopts alternative, more realistic thoughts and beliefs, which in turn lead to healthier behaviors.

The behavior part of CBT involves changing how the patient acts in order to alter their thoughts, beliefs, and feelings. Someone might be in the habit of binging on potato chips when feeling down in the dumps, which may be soothing initially but can lead to guilty feelings and greater sadness once the bag of chips is eaten. The CBT therapist would encourage the patient to alter this chip-binging habit by writing down the exact feelings experienced when the urge to eat chips strikes rather than consuming the unhealthy snack. If the patient agrees to try this change, even just once, the reduced sense of guilt may improve mood, which reinforces the new healthy behavior and breaks the cycle.

Acceptance and Commitment Therapy (ACT)

ACT involves three steps, represented by the acronym *ACT*:

1. **A**ccept your reactions and remain in the moment.
2. **C**hoose a new direction consistent with your goals and values.
3. **T**ake action or follow through with new behaviors that are more consistent with reaching your goals.

This form of therapy combines cognitive training with mindfulness techniques. The therapy ultimately aims to help people manage their uncomfortable feelings by developing psychological flexibility. Patients using this approach don't necessarily eliminate all their psychological discomfort but rather learn to accept and live with their negative emotions while making a commitment to not overreact to them. Several systematic studies indicate that ACT is effective in treating some forms of depression.

Dialectical Behavior Therapy (DBT)

This is a form of CBT that teaches skills to help depressed patients cope with stress, regulate emotions, and improve relationships. DBT also incorporates mindfulness methods and crisis coaching, which provides guidance on handling difficult situations.

One subtype of CBT is called mindfulness-based cognitive therapy, or MBCT, which was developed to help people at risk for a relapse of the depressive symptoms. The therapist focuses on increasing mindfulness, decreasing negative repetitive thoughts, or both.

Somatic Therapy

Somatic therapy focuses on the link between the mind and the body and involves both physical therapy and psychotherapy. In addition to depression, it is used to treat anxiety, grief, and addiction. The therapist helps the patient revive memories of previous traumatic experiences while paying attention to the patient's physical responses to the memories. Deep breathing, relaxation methods, meditation, massage, and other physical treatments are combined with the psychotherapy.

Psychodynamic Psychotherapy

This form of psychotherapy is based on psychoanalytic principles that assume that depression results in part from unresolved and often unconscious conflicts. Also referred to as insight-oriented psychotherapy, this approach can be very helpful in lifting feelings of depression. The therapist assists the patient in becoming aware of the thoughts and feelings that shape their behavior, and the patient is able to gain perspective and understanding of how their past influences their present feelings and behaviors. Many clinicians trained in psychodynamic theory and treatment may combine this approach with CBT and other interventions such as medication treatment.

Interpersonal Therapy

This type of therapy helps patients address their interpersonal conflicts that disrupt relationships, reduce social support, and contribute to feelings of depression. The method focuses on the patient's social roles as well as interpersonal interactions. Interpersonal therapy is usually brief and addresses the important relationships in the patient's life. The therapy may involve role-playing various scenarios to help the patient with their communication skills.

PSYCHOTHERAPIES FOR TREATING DEPRESSION

- Cognitive behavioral therapy (CBT)
- Acceptance and commitment therapy (ACT)
- Dialectical behavior therapy
- Mindfulness-based cognitive therapy
- Somatic therapy
- Psychodynamic psychotherapy
- Interpersonal psychotherapy
- Family therapy
- Group therapy
- Eye movement desensitization and reprocessing (EMDR)

Family Therapy

Many patients seek out an individual therapist for one-on-one sessions, which is comfortable for those who desire privacy about their mental experiences. It also allows the therapist to focus on the individual patient rather than other individuals.

For psychological issues that affect close relatives, however, family counseling can be helpful. When people are depressed, those around them experience those feelings too, and when the immediate family members involved meet together with a skilled

family therapist, all participants are able to understand what they contribute to the issues of the identified patient with depression.

In family therapy, relatives learn about depression
and its early warning signs. The family sessions can
also improve the patient's lifestyle habits that promote treatment compliance and healthy emotional
interactions.

Group Therapy

Group counseling involves sessions that include
patients who are depressed but are not in the same
family or do not have existing relationships outside of the treatment sessions. This form of therapy
can provide insights when patients learn how others
cope with depression. Patients develop communication skills and learn to express their problems as well
as accept criticism from others. Understanding the
experience of other depressed people struggling with
similar issues often helps patients gain self-awareness
and a new perspective.

Eye Movement Desensitization and Reprocessing (EMDR)

This form of therapy has been used primarily for the
treatment of anxiety and post-traumatic stress disorder (PTSD), but recent studies indicate its potential
for improving symptoms in different forms of depression. The treatment involves asking patients to recall

unpleasant past experiences and negative thoughts and feelings associated with those memories while at the same time performing specific eye movements. Practitioners of EMDR use various strategies to invoke the eye movements, such as asking the patient to track the light emitted as it travels back and forth along a ruler-shaped board or simply moving their finger back and forth in front of the patient's eyes. How EMDR works is not fully known, but a recent functional MRI study indicated that when research subjects make these eye movements while recalling a traumatic experience, neural activity increases between brain regions that process emotions.

CHAPTER 4

Alternative Therapies

*You know what they call alternative
medicine that's been proved to
work? Medicine.*
                    —Tim Minchin

WHEN PEOPLE SUFFERING FROM depression seek relief,
they often start by trying do-it-yourself strategies like increasing exercise or eating a healthier diet
before turning to their doctor for more conventional
treatments. Then if nothing seems to work, their next
step may be to try alternative therapies like acupuncture or reflexology.

Some depressed patients try alternative treatments first, and they often find that the treatment
relieves their symptoms. However, many alternative therapies have not been tested to determine if
they are any better than placebo, so the benefits
of the treatment may be from a placebo effect that
diminishes over time. Another issue is that using

unproven treatments often delays the use of conventional treatments that have been scientifically shown to be effective.

Some do-it-yourself strategies like meditation or yoga can also be categorized as alternative treatments for depression, and conventional medical practitioners may recommend these approaches in conjunction with evidence-based medicines or psychotherapies. When alternative approaches are used together with traditional medical interventions, they are considered complementary treatments.

These interventions are extremely popular in the Western world. An estimated 16 to 44 percent of people suffering from a mental illness use alternative therapies, and quite a few of those individuals are depressed. For patients with depression, it is estimated that 10 to 30 percent of them use alternative therapies, often without medical supervision, which may increase the likelihood of adverse effects.

When patients or families ask me about alternative therapies, I inform them of what we do and do not know about their effectiveness and safety. I encourage people to try alternative (as well as do-it-yourself) treatments, but only the ones that have a low risk and have some scientific evidence supporting their use.

DIETARY AND HERBAL SUPPLEMENTS

Valerie had been on blood-thinning medicine for several years, ever since she was diagnosed with atrial fibrillation, and she hadn't experienced any side effects. Soon after her sixtieth birthday, Valerie started worrying about her memory slips, which seemed to be getting worse every year. She'd read that vitamin E and an herb called ginkgo biloba, both sold over the counter, were good for memory, so she started taking them twice a day with meals. After a couple weeks, Valerie didn't really notice any improvement, so she upped her dosage of both.

A few days later, Valerie awoke in the night with severe stomach pain. It felt like someone was stabbing her in the abdomen with a sharp knife. She tried to eat something but couldn't keep anything down. The next day, Valerie felt a little better, so she ate a little breakfast and took her vitamins. By noon, she was doubled up in pain and vomiting blood. She managed to drive herself to the emergency room and was later admitted to the hospital for observation. Apparently, both the vitamin E and ginkgo biloba she'd been taking mega doses of contained blood-thinning elements, and when combined with Valerie's prescription blood thinners, they overwhelmed her stomach lining and caused a bleeding ulcer.

It's important to consult with your doctor before starting any type of oral alternative remedies because they may not interact well with other medicines you are taking. Blood-thinning drugs are prescribed for many conditions; however, combining them with other thinning compounds, natural or not, can lead to severe and unwanted side effects.

Also termed *nutraceuticals* or *herbal remedies*, many people use supplements and vitamins to treat their mood and memory symptoms. Dietary supplements have been regulated in the US since 1994 by the Dietary Supplement and Health Education Act, which set forth standards for manufacturers who are responsible for the truthfulness of label claims. Although several supplements have been tested and shown to be more effective than placebo, the consumer still faces challenges when deciding whether to take a particular supplement.

Quite a few people are convinced that if something is natural, it must be good for you. However, many natural supplements can cause potential side effects and can interact with other medicines to cause harm, as in Valerie's case. She might have avoided being hospitalized for a bleeding ulcer if she had discussed the risks and benefits of her alternative treatments with her physician.

Quality control of supplements is also an issue. In addition to the fact that most available supplements have not been systematically tested against a placebo treatment, some do not contain the correct amount of ingredients as advertised or may contain some contaminants.

DID YOU KNOW?

Because heightened inflammation increases the risk for depression, scientists have studied whether treatment with anti-inflammatory drugs can benefit mood. A recent systematic review of studies suggests that anti-inflammatory agents may be helpful for patients with major depression. However, not all studies are positive. For example, in 2020, Australian investigators performed a randomized, double-blind, placebo-controlled trial of aspirin. After approximately five years of follow up, aspirin was not effective in preventing depression.

Many people do not know that certain vitamin deficiencies can impact their mood. For example, an individual with a vitamin D or vitamin B_{12} deficiency may experience mood and cognitive changes, and supplementation may reverse those symptoms. There is not sufficient evidence, however, to show that supplementation with those vitamins in someone with normal vitamin blood levels will experience any improvement in mood.

When deciding which supplement may be right for you, a knowledgeable pharmacist or physician can be helpful. You might also check reliable online resources, such as the National Center for Complementary and Alternative Medicine (nccam.nih.gov) and the Natural Medicines Comprehensive Database (www.naturaldatabase.com). The following are some of the more popular supplements and herbal remedies.

St. John's Wort

Extracts from this flowering plant have been used to treat depression, anxiety, and insomnia. Its benefits may stem from action on serotonin, dopamine, and GABA brain messenger systems. Placebo-controlled trials have demonstrated its antidepressant effects in patients with mild to moderate major depression, and the effectiveness is comparable to that of conventional antidepressant medications. St. John's wort may cause side effects when taken with anti-inflammatory drugs, antidepressants, statins, or proton pump inhibitors. Possible side effects include upset stomach, headaches, skin irritation, and dry mouth.

Omega-3 Fatty Acids

Omega-3 fatty acids are polyunsaturated fatty acids derived from oily fish and certain nuts and seeds. The most common forms that have been studied in depression are eicosapentaenoic acid (EPA) and docosahexaenoic acid (DHA). The evidence for their benefits in lifting mood in depressed patients is mixed—some studies are positive while others are not, which may reflect differences in study populations, methods, and particular supplement formulations. Meta-analyses of multiple studies suggest that they are helpful for major depression symptoms, and EPA-dominated formulations seem to be more effective. Most people are able to tolerate omega-3 supplements, but possible side effects include diarrhea, nausea, and a fishy aftertaste.

SAM-e

S-adenosyl methionine (SAM-e) is present naturally in the brain, where it supports normal cellular function. It is thought to benefit mood by facilitating the transmission of neural information between cells. Systematic studies have shown that it is more effective than placebo for patients with mild to severe major depression. It may also augment the effects of antidepressant medication. Most people are able to tolerate this supplement, but potential adverse effects include upset stomach, insomnia, sweating, headaches, irritability, anxiety, and fatigue.

Acetyl-L-Carnitine

The body naturally produces acetyl-L-carnitine, which assists in transporting fatty acids to cells. A recent meta-analysis investigating its effect on depressive symptoms included twelve randomized controlled trials and concluded that acetyl-L-carnitine has a significant effect on reducing depressive symptoms compared with placebo or no intervention at all. The effect was comparable to that of antidepressant medications, and side effects were fewer.

Dehydroepiandrosterone (DHEA)

This hormone is secreted by the body's adrenal glands and is converted to male and female hormones. Results of DHEA studies have been inconsistent, although a recent investigation showed that the hormone reduced symptoms in patients with minor or major depression compared with placebo. Potential side effects include headaches, nasal congestion, fatigue, acne, and oily skin.

Folate

This B vitamin is found in leafy green vegetables, citrus fruits, and beans. Studies of folate supplements for depression have yielded mixed results. Taken by itself, folate does not appear to relieve symptoms of depression, but there is some evidence that it may augment the effects of antidepressant medications. One risk of taking folate supplements is that they could disguise symptoms of a vitamin B_{12} deficiency.

Saffron (*C. sativus*)

Saffron, which is derived from a small perennial plant, is sometimes used to lift mood. A recent meta-analysis supported its use for treating patients with mild to moderate major depression with effectiveness comparable to antidepressant medication. Potential side effects include anxiety, increased appetite, nausea, and headaches.

Lavender (*Lavandula*)

Lavender is derived from a flowing plant in the mint family. There is evidence from a randomized controlled trial that it can augment the effects of antidepressant medication. Possible side effects include nausea, confusion, and mild headaches.

Curcumin

Curcumin is a component of the spice turmeric and is a component in curried foods. It has received recent attention as a brain health supplement because of its potential for reducing mild memory symptoms in middle-aged and older adults. In addition to fighting inflammation, curcumin reduces oxidative stress that causes wear and tear on the brain. A recent systematic review of studies showed that curcumin appears to have an antidepressant effect and is well tolerated.

Probiotics

Consuming prebiotics and probiotics is an emerging strategy for improving the microbiome, the billions of microorganisms (e.g., bacteria, viruses) that occur naturally in the gut. Prebiotics are soluble fibers (e.g., onions, bananas) that assist in feeding the healthy organisms in the gut, while probiotics are microorganisms that already live within the large intestine. Consuming probiotics is thought to help healthy bacteria in the gut by reducing the number of unhealthy bacteria that heighten inflammation. Probiotics have been used to treat gastrointestinal disorders (e.g., inflammatory bowel disease, acid reflux), but some people are allergic to probiotics, which can also upset the stomach and cause bloating and constipation. Because they occur naturally in the body, they are generally safe, but checking with your doctor about potential risks is a good idea. Also, probiotic supplements are not like medications that have been cleared to treat diseases. However, some have undergone double-blind placebo-controlled studies demonstrating their effectiveness in treating certain symptoms.

In a small study, scientists found that ingesting certain probiotics did benefit a sad mood, but research on the effects of probiotics on mood is only beginning. Although the initial results are promising, we need more extensive studies to really pin down the potential benefits and risks.

Recent studies suggest that changing the makeup of the gut microbiota by consuming probiotic supplements may be helpful as an add-on to an antidepressant medicine for patients with major depressive disorder. A recent meta-analysis of five controlled trials suggests that probiotics may be useful in reducing symptoms of depression.

DIETARY AND HERBAL SUPPLEMENTS USED TO ALLEVIATE DEPRESSION

The amount of scientific evidence supporting the antidepressant benefits of these various supplements ranges from controlled studies demonstrating benefits beyond placebo to little or no evidence of any benefits at all.

Evidence for Benefits

- Acetyl-L-carnitine, curcumin, DHEA, folate, lavender, omega-3 fatty acids, probiotics, saffron, SAM-e, St. John's wort

Limited or No Scientific Evidence of Benefits

- Creatine, inositol, roseroot, theanine, tryptophan, valerian, vitamin B_6, vitamin D, yohimbe, zinc

---

NEUROMODULATION

Some forms of neuromodulation, which include technologies that change neural activity by either stimulation or suppression, have already been approved for the treatment of certain forms of depression, but others remain under investigation. These noninvasive approaches—including magnetic stimulation, ultra-sound waves, and electrical impulses—are designed to jump-start key brain neural circuits controlling mental symptoms. Some of these brain stimulation methods have minimal side effects compared to medication and tend to show positive results in treatment-resistant cases.

For patients with major depression that has not responded to antidepressant medication and those with bipolar depression, the FDA has approved repetitive transcranial magnetic stimulation (rTMS), which uses magnets to activate brain neural circuits. One limitation of this method is that it cannot reach some regions located deep within the brain.

Another option known as transcranial direct-current stimulation (tDCS) uses a simple device that involves placing electrodes on the head to excite or reduce neuronal activity. In a recent scientific review of studies, the investigators concluded that tDCS is a promising therapeutic alternative for patients with major depression, but more research is needed to confirm its efficacy.

Another technique known as low-intensity focused ultrasound pulsation (LIFUP) uses ultrasound energy pulses to excite and suppress brain cell activity. The method provides noninvasive, focused ultrasound energy through the skull and can be used with functional MRIs to target specific brain regions implicated in mood disorders and is currently under investigation for the treatment of depression.

NEUROMODULATION TECHNOLOGIES THAT MAY REDUCE DEPRESSIVE SYMPTOMS

- Repetitive transcranial magnetic stimulation (rTMS)
- Transcranial direct-current stimulation (tDCS)
- Low-intensity focused ultrasound pulsation (LIFUP)

BIOFEEDBACK AND NEUROFEEDBACK

Biofeedback and neurofeedback can train people to adjust their mood by monitoring their own physiological responses. When people are under stress, they may experience heart-rate increases, cold and clammy hands, and tense muscles, and measurements of their brain waves by electroencephalograms (EEGs) show increases in beta waves. Also, abnormal mood states lead to a shift in activity from the brain's amygdala emotional center under the temples to the frontal lobe's thinking region.

Visual or auditory input from noninvasive biofeedback sensors signal physiological changes during stress and teach the user to control their brain's activity in order to achieve and maintain a calm and focused state. Neurofeedback is a form of biofeedback that uses EEG sensors to monitor brain-wave activity. A sound or visual cue provides either positive or negative feedback. These methods have been used for a variety of mental symptoms ranging from anxiety and depression to post-traumatic stress. Although it can be helpful for some patients, it is not considered a first-line treatment for depression.

BODYWORK

Massage and other forms of bodywork can help people relax and reduce their symptoms of depression and anxiety. Anyone who has received a good massage knows how comforting it can feel, but exactly how it works to relieve mental symptoms is not entirely clear. It is possible that massage alters brain neurotransmitters involved in mood symptoms and lowers levels of stress hormones in the body. Also, if the treatment relieves pain, any mood symptom associated with that pain will likely decline.

Research has shown that moderate pressure massage provides temporary pain relief for people suffering from fibromyalgia or rheumatoid arthritis. Moderate pressure massage also alters brain-wave patterns measured by EEGs and reduces levels of the stress hormone cortisol. Studies using functional

MRIs indicate that moderate pressure massage can change brain activity in the amygdala, hypothalamus, and frontal lobe. These are all brain regions that control and regulate stress and emotion.

Many people endorse the benefits of various types of bodywork therapies, including Reiki, the Bowen technique, reflexology, aromatherapy, and chiropractic. As yet, systematic studies confirming the specific benefits of these various approaches over placebo treatments have not been confirmed. However, even without such evidence, these techniques have reportedly helped many individuals.

Acupuncture, another form of bodywork imported from the Far East and practiced for thousands of years, has been used to treat medical conditions like nausea and pain. Some scientific research does point to the benefits of acupuncture and acupressure in treating certain symptoms associated with depression, such as insomnia.

OTHER APPROACHES

Many other alternative therapies have been recommended to help people remain calm and manage their symptoms of anxiety, ranging from homeopathic treatments to prayer. Scientific evidence supporting these approaches varies, but they still seem to help some individuals.

Whole-body hyperthermia is a treatment that has been used to treat cancer, but recent research shows promise for the method's ability to reduce symptoms of depression. Investigators performed a randomized, sham-treatment controlled, double-blind investigation in patients with major depression. They found that a one-time session of heating at the level of the chest and legs until the core body temperature reached 101.3 degrees Fahrenheit led to significant reductions in symptoms of depression after six weeks. Volunteers tolerated the intervention well, with the most frequent side effects being headaches, fatigue, and dry mouth.

A meta-analysis of twenty-seven studies including nearly 1,900 men found a connection between testosterone treatments and reduced depressive symptoms. Improvements in mood were usually observed within the first six weeks of treatment. Not all men respond, and men who take testosterone have a higher risk of cardiovascular problems, like heart attacks, strokes, and death from heart disease. For men with low testosterone blood levels, however, the benefits of hormone replacement therapy may outweigh the potential risks.

I sometimes suggest that people suffering from depression try one or more alternative approach, especially the ones that have minimal risk. Systematic studies have shown that laughter or humor therapy can enhance mood and quality of life. Listening to music, spiritual pursuits, painting, various hobbies, pets, and volunteering are just some examples of potentially fun and relaxing activities that can distract us from uncomfortable emotions and help us remain calmer under stress.

ALTERNATIVE STRATEGIES FOR REDUCING DEPRESSIVE SYMPTOMS

- *Dietary and herbal supplements*
    - Acetyl-L-carnitine, curcumin, DHEA, folate, lavender, omega-3 fatty acids, probiotics, saffron, SAM-e, St. John's wort

- *Neuromodulation*
    - rTMS, tDCS, LIFUP

- *Biofeedback and neurofeedback*

- *Bodywork*
    - Massage, acupuncture, acupressure

- *Other approaches*
    - Whole-body hyperthermia, testosterone, laughter, hobbies, listening to music, prayer, spiritual pursuits, pets, volunteering

---

Many alternative treatments may help improve mood and may work well in conjunction with conventional therapies to relieve symptoms. Keep in mind that if you do pursue an alternative treatment, do not let it delay a trial of a conventional therapy that has been shown to alleviate depressive symptoms. Also, if a particular therapy sounds too good to be true, that may very well be the case. Before beginning an alternative approach, you may want to investigate whether any scientific studies have been performed to show that the approach works better than placebo, and be sure to discuss the strategy with your doctor to make sure it is safe.

CHAPTER 5

Blahs with a Cause: Situational Depression

Freud: If it's not one thing, it's your mother.

—Robin Williams

MIA WAS A SIXTY-TWO-YEAR-OLD Los Angeles real estate agent who had lived in Los Angeles with her husband, Bill, for decades. Their adult children were out of the house, and now it was just too big for the two of them. They were seriously considering downsizing to a smaller place when Bill was offered a very attractive job opportunity back east. Mia was excited because she had always wanted to live in Manhattan and had several friends there. Besides, the new job would allow Bill to retire from his current position and begin drawing on his generous pension. Also, he and Mia would have an opportunity to begin an exciting new chapter in their lives. She was excited to take a break from the grueling real estate scene in Los Angeles and live a life of leisure for a while.

When the negotiations on his new position seemed close enough that the move became a real possibility, Mia did a scouting trip and found them a great apartment in the upper west side of Manhattan. She had a great time getting the apartment together, and within a couple months, they were moved in and Bill started his new job.

Once Bill began working and was out of the apartment all day, Mia's feelings of excitement began shifting to irritability and frustration. Everything seemed harder to get done in New York, and the cold and gloomy fall weather was getting to her.

Living in the city was not nearly as glamorous as Mia had expected. Their apartment felt impossibly cramped compared with their spacious home back in Los Angeles, and her New York friends were busy with their own lives. It was great meeting up with them for dinner once in a while, but she missed her truly close friends whom she had left behind in California. And she really missed her real estate business. Sure, with Bill's higher income, she no longer needed to work, but she had never really appreciated how much she had enjoyed the social interactions and the fulfillment she experienced when she was working as a broker.

Soon her irritability changed to apathy and hopelessness. She started having crying spells when Bill was distracted by his new responsibilities and had less time for her. Many of the things that she could normally handle with ease seemed overwhelming. Fortunately, Mia was able to push through those feelings and keep her life together, but she was clearly struggling.

SYMPTOMS OF SITUATIONAL DEPRESSION

Mia was suffering from situational depression, a mental condition that involves symptoms of depression resulting from a traumatic event or major change in a person's life. Situational depression is not necessarily considered a formal psychiatric disorder, but it is an informal term that refers to a type of adjustment disorder with depressed mood or a stress response syndrome. It is often a short-term condition that occurs when a person has a hard time coping with tough situations, life changes, loss, or some other traumatic event. Symptoms usually begin within ninety days of the triggering traumatic event or major life change.

Symptoms of situational depression can be very similar to those of many other types of depression and may include sadness, helplessness, apathy, irritability, and hopelessness. Whether the individual is going through a relationship change, a loss or change of a job, or the death of a loved one, the symptoms can vary in severity and duration. Changes in appetite, sleep difficulties, and crying spells may emerge during the course of the condition.

Symptoms are typical of those that occur with any depressed state and may include hopelessness, sadness, frequent crying spells, nervousness, sleep problems, and changes in appetite.

Many different types of stress can trigger an adjustment disorder that leads to depressive symptoms. Some people experience this syndrome following the end of a relationship due to a divorce or separation. Even if the breakup is amicable, it may be hard for one or both parties to cope. The risk is greater if the relationship is a long-term one or a particularly close one. People with more extensive and meaningful social networks outside of a marriage will have an easier time adjusting to a divorce or separation. The death of a loved one, of course, can also trigger an adjustment disorder with depressed mood.

A variety of other upsets can lead to this syndrome, such as a major life change like Mia experienced. Her husband, Bill, was fortunate to have a new job, but any change in employment, whether positive or negative, can bring about unexpected emotional responses that cause stress and upset. Other possible triggers include developing a serious illness in oneself or a loved one, being a victim of a crime, having an accident, or surviving a fire, flood, earthquake, hurricane, or other natural disaster.

DO YOU HAVE SITUATIONAL DEPRESSION?

If you have gone through a difficult situation like a major life change, loss, or some other traumatic event, ask yourself if you have any of the following symptoms. If you find yourself checking off several of the boxes, you may be experiencing situational depression.

- ☐ Apathy
- ☐ Appetite changes
- ☐ Difficulty functioning in usual activities
- ☐ Fatigue
- ☐ Frequent crying spells
- ☐ Feeling overwhelmed
- ☐ Helplessness
- ☐ Hopelessness
- ☐ Increased use of alcohol
- ☐ Irritability
- ☐ Loss of concentration
- ☐ Nervousness
- ☐ Sadness
- ☐ Sleep problems
- ☐ Social withdrawal
- ☐ Suicidal thoughts

STRESSFUL LIFE EVENTS THAT CAN TRIGGER A SITUATIONAL DEPRESSION

- A serious accident
- Being a crime victim
- Death of a loved one
- Difficulties at work or getting fired
- Divorce
- Financial problems
- Getting arrested
- Having a child
- Getting married
- Legal problems
- Retirement
- Surviving a disaster like a fire, tsunami, or earthquake

DIAGNOSING SITUATIONAL DEPRESSION

These stress response syndromes can also affect nearly anyone regardless of their age, gender, race, or lifestyle. The times of life when they are most likely to strike, however, are during major life transition periods, such as adolescence, midlife, and late life.

An essential feature of an adjustment disorder is the presence of a major life stressor. The fifth edition of the American Psychiatric Association's *Diagnostic and Statistical Manual of Mental Disorders* (DSM-5) lists the following diagnostic criteria:

- Emotional or behavioral symptoms occurring within three months of a stressful event
- Greater stress than would typically be expected as a response to the stressful event or stress causing significant problems in life (e.g., relationships, work, school) or both
- Symptoms not due to another mental health disorder or normal grieving

These diagnostic criteria apply to any type of adjustment disorder, but when sadness and low mood are predominant, the disorder is specified as occurring with a depressed mood. The symptoms usually begin within three months of the stressful event and may vary in duration. The condition is considered to be acute if the symptoms last six months or less, and typically they improve if the stressor has gone away. However, at times, the condition can last longer and become persistent.

People with stress response syndrome appear similar to those with a clinical depression or major depression. The two conditions may include tearfulness, feelings of hopelessness, and loss of interest in work or activities. Major depression, however, usually involves more predominant physical symptoms such as changes in sleep patterns and appetite as well as greater severity of symptoms, such as suicidal thoughts or behavior.

An adjustment disorder or stress response syndrome also differs from post-traumatic stress disorder (PTSD). The latter is a response to a life-threatening event, and the symptoms must last at least one month in duration. In PTSD, the symptoms are usually longer lasting, while in adjustment disorders, they rarely last more than six months.

Many of the symptoms of reactive depression overlap with those of normal grief or bereavement. A key factor that helps distinguish grief from reactive depression is that people with a normal grief reaction rarely express feelings of worthlessness. Moreover, people with depressions are also more likely to have feelings of hopelessness, guilt, lack of pleasure, helplessness, and suicidal thinking.

An adjustment disorder may occur following a physical illness. A study of more than fifteen thousand patients who had suffered from a stroke showed that approximately 7 percent of them developed an adjustment disorder with depressive mood.

Because stress is so commonplace in life, the prevalence of situational depression can be high in various populations, but it is not always recognized. A study of adjustment disorders in primary care medical practices revealed that general practitioners detected only about 2 percent of cases and that nearly 40 percent of those patients who did have an adjustment disorder were taking a medicine for psychological symptoms.

If you think you have symptoms of situational depression, it may be helpful to seek medical advice. Even though a medical problem may not be the underlying cause, if not dealt with, these syndromes can worsen and develop into more serious mood disorders or contribute to a substance abuse problem.

TRYING ALTERNATIVE AND SELF-HELP STRATEGIES

Many forms of depression, including situational depression, often respond well to alternative therapies. Any number of strategies—deep-breathing exercises, biofeedback, yoga, tai chi, meditation, and hypnosis—may help reduce symptoms. In addition, the usual healthy lifestyle habits that promote brain health have been shown to reduce depressive symptoms.

Several nutritional supplements have been used to treat various forms of depression. I generally don't recommend them as first-line treatments for reactive depression because the available systematic data on their effectiveness is limited. The following are some supplements that have been shown to improve symptoms of other forms of depression, such as major depression, so it is possible that they could be helpful in adjustment disorders with depressed mood.

DIETARY SUPPLEMENTS THAT MAY BENEFIT SYMPTOMS OF REACTIVE DEPRESSION

The level of scientific evidence varies in support of the antidepressant benefits of these various supplements. Also, keep in mind that some supplements interact with medicines and can cause side effects, so always check with your doctor before beginning to use a supplement that may raise concerns.

- Acetyl-L-carnitine

- Curcumin

- DHEA

- Folate

- Lavender

- Omega-3 fatty acids

- Probiotics

- Saffron

- S-adenosyl methionine (SAM-e)

- St. John's wort

LIFESTYLE HABITS THAT MAY IMPROVE SYMPTOMS OF REACTIVE DEPRESSION

- Creating a daily walking, jogging, or other aerobic exercise routine to maintain regular physical activity that boosts mood-enhancing endorphins

- Avoiding excess consumption of alcohol and sedative medicines

- Staying socially connected

- Getting enough sleep at night and avoiding naps during the day

- Consuming a healthy diet of fish, whole grains, fruits, and vegetables

- Practicing mindful meditation, deep breathing, or other relaxation exercises

Joining a support group can help reduce feelings of isolation and provide a better understanding of your own experiences and those of others. This can be especially effective if group members have tried to cope with similar stressors and symptoms. For example, studies of adjustment disorders in patients with cancer have shown significant benefits from support groups, and individual supportive psychotherapy can be effective as well. For cancer patients with adjustment disorders, intensive emotional support has had a positive impact on survival rates for malignant melanoma, non–small cell lung cancer, leukemia, and gastrointestinal tract cancers, but results for patients with breast cancer are mixed.

Remaining socially connected with empathic friends and relatives is always helpful in gaining perspective on depressive symptoms and avoiding feelings of isolation.

Mindfulness, meditation, and relaxation methods have been shown to improve mood in a variety of depressive syndromes. A recent study found that mindfulness training was associated with improved psychological symptoms, quality of life, and mindfulness skills in patients with adjustment disorders. A randomized controlled trial of mindfulness-based group therapy was shown to be as effective as individual-based cognitive behavioral therapy (CBT) for primary care patients with depressive forms of adjustment disorders. Yoga meditation methods also have been shown to be effective in improving symptoms of adjustment disorders with anxiety and depression.

CONVENTIONAL THERAPIES

The most common conventional strategy for treating adjustment disorders and related stress response syndromes is psychotherapy. Talking therapies can help people gain insight into how a particular stressor has impacted their lives and can provide better ways to cope with stress in general to avoid future episodes.

Although therapy for situational depression can be very effective, a barrier can be the patient's resistance to getting help. Many people with this condition feel that it is not severe enough to warrant professional help. Or they may feel that it is a stigma or a sign of weakness that they cannot solve their problems on their own. However, untreated situational depression can get worse and may even worsen physical illnesses, such as heart disease and bowel disorders.

Making the first appointment to see a mental health professional is the first step to getting help. If the patient's personal physician or a trusted friend or family member can explain how therapy works and how its purpose is to help and not harm people, that can help a resistant patient get started. When I meet people who are hesitant, I try to explore what is holding them back. Often the conversation can help them realize how their concerns or fears are unfounded.

If a particular stressor, such as the loss of a job, is alleviated because the patient was able to find new employment, then symptoms are likely to remit. But that is not always the case, such as with a patient suffering from terminal cancer. Psychotherapy to address the psychological meaning of the stressor along with social support can certainly improve quality of life and mitigate symptoms.

Several types of psychotherapy have been used for adjustment disorders with depressed mood, including CBT and interpersonal therapy, which have been shown to be effective. These approaches can lower the risk for suicidal thinking and self-harm behaviors.

Some CBT interventions have been adjusted to target specific stressors such as cancer or burglary. They also have been adapted to assist particular populations ranging from military recruits to older adults. A systematic review of the effectiveness of interventions that help adjustment-disordered patients return to work concluded that general CBT interventions did not significantly reduce time until return to work compared with no intervention. However, problem-solving therapy did improve partial return to work after a year compared to a control condition. This is a form of CBT designed to improve someone's ability to cope with stressful life experiences.

Many CBT therapists will add behavioral activation as a way to help the patient engage more often in enjoyable activities as well as improve their problem-solving skills. This approach becomes prescriptive in the sense that the therapist actually helps the patient schedule particular enjoyable experiences. Previous studies that included interventions that encourage patients with adjustment disorder to return to work had activating components.

Many patients gain insight into the triggers for their stress response from psychodynamic therapies, which help them explore how current stressors stir up unresolved feelings from the past. Research has shown that short-term psychodynamic psychotherapy, which lasts from six to nine months, will reduce symptoms. Other studies indicate that interpersonal psychotherapy is effective as well. This form of therapy is based on the idea that personal relationships are at the core of psychological problems and thus focuses on the patient's relationships with others.

Eye movement desensitization and reprocessing (EMDR) is another therapeutic strategy showing promise in treating adjustment disorders with depressive features. The treatment involves asking patients to recall unpleasant past experiences and negative thoughts and feelings associated with those memories while at the same time performing specific eye movements. Patients with adjustment disorder with mixed anxiety and depressed mood have experienced clinically significant improvements at follow-up, but studies of patients with only depressed mood without anxiety symptoms have not improved as well.

Other approaches that show promise include eHealth interventions, which involve the use of unguided self-help protocols delivered online. Such approaches allow for early intervention after the experience of a stressful life event that could trigger an adjustment disorder.

If symptoms are severe enough, medications such as antidepressants and antianxiety agents may

---

MEDICATIONS THAT MAY ALLEVIATE REACTIVE DEPRESSION SYMPTOMS

- Minor tranquilizers or benzodiazepines for anxiety symptoms

    Examples: alprazolam (Xanax), chlordiazepoxide (Librium), diazepam (Valium), and lorazepam (Ativan)

- Buspirone (Buspar)

- Antidepressants

    Examples: Zoloft, Prozac, escitalopram (Lexapro), duloxetine (Cymbalta), venlafaxine (Effexor XR), and paroxetine (Paxil)

---

be used to temporarily reduce them. Because non-pharmacological approaches seem to be effective in addressing the underlying psychological issues that trigger symptoms, medicine is often used in combination with psychotherapy, self-help approaches, and lifestyle changes.

If you believe you have a reactive depression that is disrupting your life, know that these conditions often respond to interventions. Keep in mind that traditional treatments and alternative therapies can be effective in alleviating symptoms and combining several approaches can make the difference between a life of persistent mental anguish or one that is fulfilling and symptom-free.

CHAPTER 6

Blues That Come and Go: Clinical Depression

Apparently, rock bottom has a basement.

—Anonymous

ADAM, A FORTY-SEVEN-YEAR-OLD ADVERTISING executive, arose at 5:30 in the morning as usual. He loved getting his morning run out of the way before his wife and kids awoke. Adam quietly brushed his teeth and tiptoed downstairs to put on running shoes but broke a lace. He rifled through every junk drawer in the kitchen and service porch but couldn't find a spare shoelace to save his life. Frustrated, Adam sat down at the table, and all of a sudden, he started to cry. He surprised himself—who the heck cries over a broken shoelace? However, it was like floodgates had opened, and Adam couldn't stop his tears for several minutes.

He pulled himself together and started breakfast for the family because he heard them stirring upstairs. When his wife, Pam, came down and saw his red eyes, she asked him what was wrong. Adam said he was just tired and had decided not to run that day.

The next morning, his alarm went off at 5:30 again, but for the first time in years, Adam didn't feel like running. He stayed in bed and went back to sleep. Pam woke him up at 7:45 and said he was going to miss his train if he didn't get going.

Adam felt lethargic all day and couldn't really focus on the campaign he was working on. He thought he might be coming down with a bug and left work early. Pam checked his temperature, which was normal, but knew how unlike Adam it was to be so mopey and tired all day. She insisted he go to bed early; hopefully, he'd be better in the morning.

Adam skipped his run again the next day and felt so fatigued he didn't want to get out of bed. He hadn't slept well and had no appetite for breakfast. Pam called their internist and made an appointment for Adam that afternoon.

The doctor did a full work-up but couldn't find an explanation for Adam's fatigue, moodiness, and distraction. The doctor suggested Adam call a psychiatrist he knew and perhaps go in for a chat. Adam laughed and said he was tired, not crazy, thanks.

When he laughingly told Pam that their internist suggested a psychiatrist, Pam thought it was a good idea. Maybe a psychiatrist could help Adam figure out what was causing his symptoms, and it couldn't hurt. Adam said he didn't have time to start all that, and he'd be fine in a day or two. After a few more days of moping around, Adam agreed to make an appointment with the shrink.

Adam waited outside of Dr. Preston's office until she opened the door and invited him in. He was a bit nervous at first, but the doctor put him at ease—she was friendly and easy to talk to.

She learned that his doctor could find nothing medically wrong with him, and she asked for more details about his current symptoms and his past history. When she continued to probe, Dr. Preston learned that Adam had both mood symptoms (tearfulness, loss of interest in his usual activities) as well as physical symptoms (insomnia, fatigue, low appetite). Adam remembered feeling somewhat like this in college after he sprained his ankle and had to forgo his daily run for a few weeks. He'd attributed that episode to low energy from a lack of exercise.

When Dr. Patterson found out that Adam's father had experienced similar episodes wherein he seemed to be withdrawn and lethargic, sometimes for months, she shared what she thought was going on. She believed that Adam had a relatively common condition known as major depression. It is usually episodic and sometimes begins without any particular trigger or stressful event. It likely results from imbalances of normal brain chemical messengers. She explained how the condition can be inherited to some extent, and it was possible that his father had a similar predisposition to his own.

Adam was a bit surprised, but he actually felt relieved. Someone finally seemed to understand what was going on with him. He felt even better when the psychiatrist told him that his condition usually responds well to treatment and that she was confident that she would be able to help him.

Adam is one of the millions of people who suffer from major depressive episodes, a condition that is also called clinical depression. A recent national survey of more than thirty-five thousand adults found that over a twelve-month period, major depressive disorder afflicts more than 10 percent of the population. Over a lifetime, that prevalence is nearly 21 percent.

Adam was fortunate in that he had a relatively mild form of the illness and had suffered only a few episodes, but this condition can be disabling and even life-threatening if left untreated. Depressive episodes can last for months or even years and may seem to occur out of nowhere, which is what Adam experienced. Sometimes, however, there can be a triggering event. Adam may have experienced a mild episode during college that was triggered by his temporary inability to exercise due to a sprained ankle.

Although people tend to think of mental health problems like depression as purely psychological ones, they clearly have physiological underpinnings. These are often manifested by the physical symptoms that are typical of major depression.

WHAT IS MAJOR DEPRESSION?

It's normal for anyone to experience ups and downs on a typical day. Minor upsets can bring about feelings of sadness or discouragement. Major depression, however, is more than just a mild mood alteration; it consists of a syndrome of symptoms that have been shown to respond to specific conventional and lifestyle interventions.

When I was training in psychiatry, I learned an easy mnemonic to help me remember the clinical features of major depression: SIG E CAPS. That was shorthand for when to prescribe the energy capsules (*SIG* is short for the Latin *signetur*, or "let it be labeled," which doctors write on prescription pads). Each of those letters stands for one of the symptoms: *S* for a sleep problem; *I* for loss of interest; *G* for feelings of guilt; *E* for low energy levels; *C* for poor concentration abilities; *A* for loss of appetite; *P* for psychomotor disturbance, meaning the patient is slower either

DO YOU HAVE MAJOR DEPRESSION?

Check off each of the symptoms you may be experiencing. If you find that you are checking three or more, you may be suffering from major depression.

☐ Appetite change, weight change, or both

☐ Feelings of guilt

☐ Loss of interest in usual activities

☐ Low energy levels

☐ Slowed physical or mental movement

☐ Poor ability to concentrate

☐ Sadness, tearfulness

☐ Sleep disturbance (insomnia or hypersomnia)

☐ Thoughts of suicide or passive thoughts of death

physically or mentally or both; and the second *S* for thoughts of suicide. Sometimes patients don't have active suicidal thinking but passive thoughts of death (e.g., "I would be fine if I died naturally right now."). These symptoms are also part of the definition of major depressive disorder described in the fifth edition of the American Psychiatric Association's *Diagnostic and Statistical Manual of Mental Disorders* (DSM-5).

DIAGNOSTIC FEATURES OF MAJOR DEPRESSIVE DISORDER

According to the American Psychiatric Association's DSM-5, the following features must be present for a diagnosis of major depression. The individual must have five or more symptoms over the course of the same two-week period. Moreover, at least one of the symptoms needs to be either a depressed mood or a loss of interest or pleasure (also known as anhedonia). These symptoms include the following:

- A depressed mood that lasts most of the day and occurs almost every day
- An extreme loss of interest or pleasure in most undertakings most of the day and almost every day
- Weight loss or weight gain or a decline or increase in appetite
- Thinking and physical movement that is slowed down (known as psychomotor retardation)
- Low energy levels almost every day
- Feelings of worthlessness or extreme guilt nearly every day
- Trouble thinking or concentrating, or indecisiveness, nearly every day
- Repeated thoughts of death or suicidal thinking

In addition, these symptoms must be distressing or interfere with the patient's social, occupational, or other important areas of functioning. The symptoms also cannot be caused by substance abuse or another medical condition.

The onset of a first episode of major depression can occur at any time in life ranging from adolescence to older age. Women are at greater risk than men: approximately one-third of all women will develop a major depressive episode at some point in life. People with low self-esteem and who have trouble coping with stress are also at risk.

Some women develop a related condition known as premenstrual dysphoric disorder, wherein they have severe symptoms of depression, irritability, and tension about a week before menstruation begins. They often have mood swings, irritability, or anger along with a depressed mood and anxiety. In addition to reduced interest in usual activities, they may experience trouble concentrating, fatigue, insomnia, and appetite changes. The symptoms begin about a week before the start of menstruation and improve at the onset of menses.

Men are less likely to seek help for their depression than are women. They may not actually feel sad or blue but instead become irritable and angry and abuse alcohol and drugs to reduce their symptoms. Suppressing such negative feelings can lead to violent behavior and thus increase their risk for suicide or homicide.

Adam had a family history of possible major depression. Family and genetic studies indicate a high degree of heritability—if you have a parent or sibling with major depression, your risk of developing it is about 40 percent. However, environmental factors can contribute to depression risk as well. People who have been exposed to violence, neglect, abuse, or poverty have an increased risk for developing major depression.

The condition overlaps with grief reactions following the death of a loved one or the loss of a job or a divorce or separation. Many people who are in bereavement describe their feelings as sad and depressed. Grieving individuals often withdraw socially as many depressed people do. However, in a grief reaction, the sad feelings come and go in waves and are often mixed with fond memories, whereas with depression, the sadness or loss of interest persists for at least two weeks.

Also, grieving individuals usually maintain a sense of self-esteem, which may be diminished in patients with major depression. People in grief may consider "joining" their deceased loved one, but depressed people consider actually ending their lives to avoid their pain.

For your doctor to make an accurate diagnosis of major depression, it is important to ensure that a medical condition is not causing the symptoms, since many physical illnesses and medications can lead to mood changes. This process will involve a review of your medicines with your doctor and a series of blood tests if they have not already been done.

PHYSICAL CONDITIONS ASSOCIATED WITH DEPRESSION

- Alzheimer's disease

- Arthritis

- Autoimmune disease (lupus, rheumatoid arthritis)

- Cancer

- Chronic pain such as back pain, headaches

- Diabetes

- Heart disease, heart attacks

- Medicines for acne, pain, allergies, blood pressure, insomnia, and anxiety as well as anticonvulsants, oral contraceptives, and antibiotics

- Multiple sclerosis

- Parkinson's disease

- Seizures

- Strokes

- Traumatic brain injury

- Use of alcohol and recreational drugs

DEPRESSION IN OLDER ADULTS

When an older adult becomes depressed, it can be more difficult to recognize than when younger individuals get depressed. Older depressed patients sometimes don't even feel sad or blue but instead complain about physical problems, such as back pain or headaches. In fact, there often tends to be a focus on physical rather than psychological symptoms, and mental health professionals have termed this condition *masked depression*.

Some of today's seniors grew up in a time when seeing a psychiatrist or psychologist meant you were somehow "crazy," so they may express a lot of resistance to accepting a diagnosis and treatment for something that is "only in your mind." This is particularly challenging when the patient is not perceiving any mental symptoms but rather losing weight due to a poor appetite, having trouble sleeping, and focusing on symptoms of chronic pain.

When I work with such resistant older adults, I discuss their concerns about the physical symptoms they are experiencing and try to avoid labeling them as "depressed" but instead talk about how I can help them feel better. If I think an antidepressant may reducc their symptoms, I talk about the antidepressant medicine being found to help with not just depression but the kinds of symptoms and concerns they have been experiencing. Many of these patients will be willing to admit that they worry about their symptoms even if they don't actually feel sad or depressed.

Older depressed patients also frequently focus on their poor concentration abilities, and at times, their depression may appear very much like a major cognitive problem such as dementia. This is often called pseudodementia or dementia syndrome of depression. This diagnostic dilemma is further complicated by the fact that many patients who have Alzheimer's dementia—up to a third in some studies—will develop depression. Also, patients who have experienced a stroke or a series of small strokes in the brain have a higher risk for developing depression.

CONVENTIONAL THERAPIES FOR MAJOR DEPRESSION

The good news is that major depression is very responsive to treatment. The majority of patients who receive proper treatment respond well, and nearly all of them gain some relief from their symptoms.

A variety of psychotherapies—including cognitive behavioral therapy (CBT), psychodynamic therapy, and interpersonal psychotherapy—have been found to be effective in treating major depression. The rates of remission with cognitive therapy or medication alone can be as high as 50 percent, but combining medication treatment with talking therapies is generally more effective.

MEDICATION TREATMENTS FOR MAJOR DEPRESSION

- *Antidepressants.* SSRIs and SNRIs are first-line treatments and may take weeks or months to become effective. Tricyclic antidepressants are also effective in many cases. Monoamine oxidase inhibitors (MAOIs) are effective but require dietary restrictions to avoid serious side effects. Examples include citalopram (Celexa), fluvoxamine (Luvox), paroxetine (Paxil), imipramine (Tofranil), venlafaxine (Effexor), and phenelzine (Nardil).

- *Minor tranquilizers or benzodiazepines.* These can help reduce the anxiety feelings that sometimes accompany major depression but are not first-line treatments. They can become habit-forming and may cause side effects when used with alcohol. These medicines need to be used with caution and only when symptoms are incapacitating. Examples include alprazolam (Xanax), clonazepam (Klonopin), diazepam (Valium), and lorazepam (Ativan).

Several medicines have been shown to be effective, including antidepressant medicines such as selective serotonin reuptake inhibitors (SSRIs; e.g., Prozac,

Zoloft), serotonin norepinephrine reuptake inhibitors (SNRIs; e.g., Cymbalta, Effexor), and tricyclic antidepressants (e.g., Pamelor, Tofranil). These medicines appear to exert their effects by alterations in the levels of neurotransmitters like serotonin, which are implicated in mood disturbances. Antianxiety medicines such as benzodiazepines may also be prescribed to reduce accompanying anxiety symptoms.

DID YOU KNOW?

- Imbalances in brain messengers or neurotransmitters such as dopamine, serotonin, and norepinephrine have been linked to mood regulation. Too much or too little of these neurotransmitters in your brain can contribute to symptoms of depression.

- Changes in levels of hormones that occur during pregnancy, menstruation, or menopause or from thyroid abnormalities could contribute to depression.

Not everyone responds to an antidepressant treatment, and even if the medicine is effective, it can sometimes take months to observe benefits. However, a recent study suggested that positive alterations in cognition may predict responses. The investigators found a relatively consistent link between a positive antidepressant response and early improvement in

cognitive abilities. The patients who started to process information more accurately began to enjoy a lift
in their mood.

Psychotherapy can be effective in reducing symptoms even if there is no obvious environmental trigger for the depression. Therapeutic methods like
CBT can help patients identify thoughts and feelings that lead to maladaptive behaviors that worsen
symptoms and help them learn more effective
responses. This can be done through individual or
group sessions, can be delivered in weekly sessions,
and can reduce symptoms within months. Many
patients find psychodynamic psychotherapy useful
in helping them avoid maladaptive behaviors that
complicate their symptoms and functioning. Other
approaches like family therapy and supportive psychotherapy can help patients deal with interpersonal
and other psychological stressors that contribute to
symptoms. Numerous positive randomized controlled trials have demonstrated the effectiveness of
these different therapeutic interventions in various
forms of depression.

TREATMENT-RESISTANT DEPRESSION

If you are being treated for depression and your symptoms have not improved, you may have treatment-
resistant depression. Your doctor may wish to allow

your medicine more time to work or switch medicines. Also, it is possible that the medication dose is
too low. Another strategy is to add a medicine to augment the antidepressant response. Sometimes lithium or thyroid medication is added in small doses.

Some people do not respond to their medication
because they metabolize certain antidepressants so
rapidly that the medicine is ineffective. A genetic test
can determine if that is an issue for you, and that
test will help guide your doctor to choose a more
effective one.

Other strategies for addressing treatment-resistant
depression include electroconvulsive therapy (ECT),
transcranial magnetic stimulation (TMS), and vagus
nerve stimulation. The most commonly used somatic
therapy for treatment-resistant major depression is
ECT, which has been shown to be both safe and effective, despite the dramatic negative depictions of ECT
in the media. Electrodes are placed over the temples, and a brief electrical charge is applied while the
patient is under anesthesia. The treatments are often
given three days a week for several weeks, and antidepressant medicines are given for the maintenance
of the antidepressant effect thereafter. Patients can
experience mild amnesia, but it is only temporary.
The anesthetic is very brief, and the treatment only
lasts a few minutes. ECT is so safe and effective that
it is often given on an outpatient basis.

Repetitive transcranial magnetic stimulation (rTMS) is an FDA-approved somatic therapy for treatment-resistant major depression. This is a non-invasive treatment involving the use of a magnetic field that alters brain neural circuits. A recent systematic review of multiple studies comparing rTMS to sham treatment has demonstrated its effectiveness for treating major depression.

Another treatment is called vagus nerve stimulation. This method uses electrical impulses to stimulate the vagus nerve and intervention requires the placement of a device that is implanted in the chest with a wire that sends impulses to the vagus nerve in the neck. These electrical signals travel along the vagus nerve to the mood centers of the brain.

ALTERNATIVE STRATEGIES
FOR MAJOR DEPRESSION

Some of the same nutritional supplements that might reduce symptoms in any form of depression may also help patients with major depression, although the evidence for their benefits may vary. Many alternative interventions have been used to successfully augment the benefits of conventional treatments.

ALTERNATIVE MAJOR DEPRESSION INTERVENTIONS

- *Dietary and herbal supplements*
  - ○ Acetyl-L-carnitine, curcumin, DHEA, folate, lavender, omega-3 fatty acids, probiotics, saffron, SAM-e, St. John's wort
- *Biofeedback and neurofeedback*
- *Bodywork*
  - ○ Massage, acupuncture, acupressure
- *Other approaches*
  - ○ Exercise, meditation, yoga, listening to music, pets, volunteering

Studies have shown that regular exercise can reduce symptoms of depression, and many patients with depression report feeling better when they remain physically active. Proper nutrition may also reduce the frequency and degree of symptoms. Excessive amounts of caffeine, alcohol, or even monosodium glutamate (MSG) may increase symptoms of anxiety and worsen mood. Some strategies to keep in mind include the following:

- *Remain patient.* The treatments don't work over-night. Avoid skipping therapy sessions and take your medication as directed. If you are experiencing side effects, reach out to your doctor.

- *Avoid alcohol and recreational drugs.* Sometimes patients with major depression try to reduce their symptoms with alcohol and drugs, but this strategy eventually worsens symptoms. Moreover, alcohol can decrease the effectiveness of antidepressant medications.

- *Manage stress.* Everyday stressors will make symptoms worse, so make a habit of practicing stress-reduction methods like yoga, tai chi, meditation, mindfulness, progressive muscle relaxation, or journaling.

- *Get enough sleep.* Learn how to get a good night's sleep without sleeping pills. CBT for insomnia has been shown to be effective, as are other methods (regular bedtimes, avoiding liquids and caffeine in the evenings) that help you feel rested the next day.

- *Exercise every day.* This will boost your body's natural antidepressant, endorphin. It will help you feel more relaxed in the evening as well, which will make it easier to fall asleep and stay asleep.

Knowledge of major depression, what it is, and how to treat it can be comforting for many patients who realize they no longer have to fear that they are losing control. Many feel reassured when they understand that brain changes are driving their symptoms and that those symptoms will pass if they remain patient, get the right treatment, and simply wait them out.

Major depression is a common condition that, if left untreated, can lead to significant complications and even death. It is more common in people suffering from medical illnesses. Even though patients respond well to combined medication treatment and psychotherapy, the initial treatment plan may not work, so it is important to be patient and work closely with your doctor to find the optimal therapy.

Healthy lifestyle strategies also help reduce symptoms. It is important that patients with severe depression or suicidal thoughts, as well as people who have failed to respond to several antidepressant medications, see a psychiatrist for more targeted interventions. Finally, if anyone mentions suicidal thinking, it is important to ensure that the individual is safe, which may require immediate professional attention.

CHAPTER 7

Swinging High and Low: Manic Depression

You have to fight a battle more than once to win it.

—Margaret Thatcher

ISABELLA, A TWENTY-EIGHT-YEAR-OLD NOVELIST working on her second book, had been in psychotherapy for about five years, but her longtime therapist retired several months back. Although he gave her a few names of alternate psychiatrists to call, Isabella felt so good at the time that she stuck the referral list in a drawer somewhere and decided to go it alone. She was being very productive at work—completing at least a chapter a week—and she couldn't remember her last bout of writer's block.

A couple weeks later, however, Isabella began feeling tired and distracted after working for just an hour or so. The more she thought about working on the

book and its approaching deadline, the more anxious she became and the less work she got done. She
couldn't sleep through the night, and her appetite
became nonexistent. Isabella thought about quitting
the stupid book and giving back the advance, but she
knew her agent and publisher would be mad at her.
She wished she could talk to her old psychiatrist and
then remembered the list of referrals he had given
her. After searching the apartment, she found the
list and called the first name. She was able to get an
appointment for the following week.

The morning of the appointment, Isabella realized
that she was feeling good again—fantastic, actually.
She was writing like crazy, the ideas were flowing, and she really didn't need much sleep at night.
She considered canceling the appointment with
the new shrink but decided to go meet him just in case
she needed someone in the future.

When Isabella met her new psychiatrist, she
described how good she was feeling. She was knock-
ing out chapters on her new novel and had finally
organized her closet and her office, but she was also
feeling restless. When the doctor asked about her
medications, Isabella admitted that she was not taking her medicines since her prescriptions had run
out and she hadn't had a chance to refill them.

Isabella's previous doctor had diagnosed her with
bipolar disorder, and generally, she did okay with it.
However, when she got manic, she would often write

straight through the night, and when she read it the next day, most of it made no sense. These episodes were usually followed by deep depressions, when Isabella would lose all motivation, feel hopeless, and occasionally have suicidal thoughts.

After listening to Isabella's story, her new doctor suggested that in addition to taking her lithium and antidepressant medicines, she should start attending a local support group with other people her age who were dealing with the same diagnosis. He also wanted her to start coming in each week to talk about how she was feeling.

They arranged an appointment for the next week, but when Isabella returned, the doctor became concerned about her behavior: she had pressured speech and appeared euphoric. Isabella laughed and said she was just fine now that she was taking her meds. But after a few minutes, she became irate and started yelling at him—why didn't he trust her and believe that she was taking her meds? She started pacing the room and said that if she was such a liar, maybe she should just end her life. With that, her doctor knew that she needed to come into the hospital for her safety and the stabilization of her medications.

Although bipolar disorder can have devastating effects on patient's lives, it can be treated effectively. When patients are in a manic state, they are energetic and euphoric and often feel omnipotent. Because the mania can feel so good to patients, they often stop

taking their mood-stabilizing medicine. Unfortunately, if the mania escalates, patients can develop
rapid speech, hallucinations, delusions, and aggres-
sive behavior.

This illness, which has been called both bipolar
disorder and manic depressive illness, afflicts about
2 percent of the population and is characterized by
episodes of elevated and depressed moods that disrupt the patient's ability to function normally.

Bipolar disorder is a chronic condition that often
begins in childhood or adolescence. There are two
major subtypes: Isabella had subtype I, which is
characterized by full-blown manic episodes. When
patients with bipolar II experience elevated mood
episodes, their symptoms are not as extreme and are
referred to as hypomania. However, the depressive
episodes of bipolar I and II can be quite similar.

These alternating high and low periods are separated by periods of relative normalcy described as
euthymia, but patients may continue to have difficulties functioning during euthymic periods.

DO YOU HAVE BIPOLAR DISORDER?

People with manic-depressive illness experience many of
the following symptoms that are characterized by discrete
episodic changes in mood, thinking, and behavior. Check off
any of the following that might apply to you. If you check

off three or more, you may be suffering from this condition and should consult with a psychiatrist for an accurate diagnosis and treatment plan.

- ☐ Depressed mood and loss of interest in usual activities
- ☐ Difficulty sleeping or sleeping too much and feeling tired during the day
- ☐ Distortions in thought such as delusions (false fixed beliefs)
- ☐ Extreme productivity
- ☐ Feelings of guilt or worthlessness
- ☐ Grandiose thinking
- ☐ Hearing voices or seeing things that are not really there (hallucinations)
- ☐ Inability to concentrate and focus attention
- ☐ Irritability, anger, or aggression
- ☐ Talking more than usual or feeling pressure to continue talking
- ☐ Multitasking yet having difficulty getting anything accomplished
- ☐ Racing thoughts
- ☐ Risk-taking behaviors
- ☐ Slowed thinking or body movements
- ☐ Suicidal thinking

Around 80 to 90 percent of patients with manic-depressive illness have other family members with the disorder or with major depression. Their children have a 5 to 15 percent risk of developing the condition, indicating a strong genetic component.

These patients are also predisposed to other mental health problems. Anxiety disorder, post-traumatic stress disorder (PTSD), attention deficit hyperactivity disorder (ADHD), personality disorder, and alcohol or drug dependence all occur at higher rates in patients with bipolar disorder. They are also at risk for medical illnesses, such as cardiovascular and metabolic disorders.

DIAGNOSING BIPOLAR DISORDER

Bipolar disorder occurs in three different forms, and all of them involve alterations in mood as well as levels of energy and activity. The elated periods involve feelings of euphoria as well as irritability, while the low episodes are typical of any depression, with sadness, hopelessness, and indifference. The first step in making a diagnosis is determining the subtype:

- *Bipolar I:* at least a week of a manic episode. Sometimes these episodes can be mixed and include depressive symptoms as well.

- *Bipolar II:* a pattern that includes depressive episodes, but the elated periods are hypomanic ones, so they are not as extreme as with a full-blown manic episode.
- *Cyclothymic disorder or cyclothymia:* episodes of hypomania and depressive symptoms that have been going on for two or more years. The symptoms are less severe than in bipolar II.

In arriving at a diagnosis of manic-depressive disorder, the doctor needs to differentiate the illness from other mental disorders that may present with similar symptoms. Patients with bipolar I may lose touch with reality during their episodes, so they may hear or see things that are not really there (hallucinations) or have false beliefs that people are after them or that some alien force is taking over their mind and body (delusions).

In a manic state, the patient may believe they are famous or have special powers, whereas when depressed, they may have delusions of being penniless or of having a fatal illness. During such psychotic states, a patient with manic-depressive illness may seem to have schizophrenia, but the symptoms of schizophrenia are generally more severe. In addition to psychotic symptoms, patients with schizophrenia have social withdrawal and disorganized thinking as well as difficulty caring for themselves.

DIAGNOSTIC FEATURES OF
MANIA AND HYPOMANIA

Specific diagnostic criteria have been described in the American Psychiatric Association's *Diagnostic and Statistical Manual of Mental Disorders* (DSM) and include the following features.

Manic Episode

A. Distinct abnormal and persistent episodes of heightened, expansive, or irritable mood along with elevated goal-directed activity or energy. The episodes must last a week or more and be present most of the time.

B. During these periods, three or more of the following must be present:

- Elevated self-esteem or grandiosity
- Less need for sleep
- Talking more than usual or feeling pressure to continue talking
- Racing thoughts
- Distractibility
- Greater goal-directed activity or purposeless agitation
- Risk-taking behavior such as buying sprees, sexual indiscretions, or foolish business investments

C. Episodes interfere with social or occupational functioning or lead to hospitalization for safety.

D. Symptoms are not attributable to drug abuse, medication, or a medical condition.

Hypomanic Episode

A. Distinct abnormal and persistent episodes of heightened, expansive, or irritable mood along with elevated goal-directed activity or energy. The episodes must last four days or more and be present most of the time.

B. During these periods, three or more of the following symptoms must be present:
- Elevated self-esteem or grandiosity
- Less need for sleep
- Talking more than usual or feeling pressure to continue talking
- Racing thoughts
- Distractibility
- Greater goal-directed activity or purposeless agitation
- Risk-taking behavior such as buying sprees, sexual indiscretions, or foolish business investments

C. Episodes interfere with social or occupational functioning.

D. Symptoms are observable by others.

E. Episodes are not severe enough to impair social or occupational functioning or require hospitalization.

F. Symptoms are not attributable to drug abuse, medication, or a medical condition.

Some patients have symptoms of both a mood (or affective) disorder and schizophrenia, which is a condition known as schizoaffective disorder.

Sometimes manic-depressive patients may be confused with patients with personality disorders. A personality disorder is characterized by a consistent pattern of thoughts, feelings, and behaviors that disrupts everyday functioning. These maladaptive patterns tend to be stable and persistent, whereas bipolar disorder is more of an episodic illness.

Patients with frontotemporal dementia early in the course of their illness may present like a patient with bipolar disorder. Patients with frontotemporal dementia may initially have behavioral or language disturbances without cognitive symptoms. A variety of other conditions may appear as manic-depressive illness, including obsessive compulsive disorder, anxiety disorders, ADHD, and substance abuse. A careful evaluation by a mental health professional can effectively differentiate these illnesses, which will guide the practitioner in determining a targeted treatment strategy.

CONVENTIONAL THERAPIES FOR BIPOLAR DISORDER

Medications are the first line of treatment for manic episodes. The episodic highs have been shown to be

controlled with mood-stabilizing drugs, such as lithium (Eskalith or Lithobid). In addition to controlling
the elevated mood, lithium can help the patient sleep
better and regulate their behavior more effectively.
Common side effects of lithium include weight gain,
memory and concentration problems, tremors, and
fatigue, so lithium treatment needs to be monitored
closely. Blood tests allow the doctor to ensure that
lithium levels are in a safe and therapeutic range.

Antiseizure drugs that are also used to stabilize
mood include valproate (Depakote), lamotrigine
(Lamictal), and carbamazepine (Tegretol). The doctor may prescribe an antiseizure medicine alone or
along with lithium. Anticonvulsant medicines work
by calming hyperactivity in the brain. It may also be
necessary to monitor the blood levels of these medicines. Possible side effects of anticonvulsants include
fatigue, nausea, tremors, and weight gain.

In severe cases of mania or depression, electroconvulsive therapy (ECT) may be recommended.
When I was in psychiatry training, I treated a patient
who was in such a severe manic state that she had
stopped talking and had been catatonic for nearly
a month. Medication had no effect, but ECT treatments quickly brought her back to a euthymic mental
state.

Patients who have bipolar disorder may be taking
antidepressant medications for their depressive episodes, but these medicines can sometimes induce a

manic state, so it would be important to discontinue antidepressants if mania is the primary problem.

THE BIPOLAR BRAIN

Clearly, patients with bipolar disorder have difficulties regulating their emotions and behaviors. Neuroimaging studies of these patients have demonstrated neural circuitry alterations in brain regions that control these functions, including areas of the frontal lobe (also known as the thinking brain) and the amygdala, a brain area that controls emotional responses. Research on brain changes following treatment with mood-stabilizing medicines show improvements in both the structure and functioning of these brain regions. Some studies of brain function indicate that regions involved in emotional reward processing show heightened or reduced neural activation depending on whether patients are in a manic or depressed state. When manic or hypomanic, patients are keenly focused on emotionally rewarding behaviors, whereas their depressed states are ones of retreat and lack of interest in external emotional gratifications.

If the patient has psychotic symptoms, then the doctor may prescribe an antipsychotic drug, which exerts its effect by altering the function of brain neurotransmitters like dopamine and serotonin. Because lithium can take days to weeks to have an effect, antipsychotics may be used initially to quickly control symptoms. Examples of these medicines include aripiprazole (Abilify), lurasidone (Latuda), quetiapine (Seroquel), and olanzapine (Zyprexa). These medicines may cause weight gain, high cholesterol levels, and high blood sugar levels. Common side effects include drowsiness, weight gain, and dry mouth.

TREATMENTS FOR BIPOLAR DISORDER

- Medication
  - Mood stabilizers
  - Antianxiety medicines
  - Antidepressants
  - Antipsychotic medications
- ECT
- Psychotherapy
  - Family therapy
  - Psychoeducation
- Interpersonal therapy

Antianxiety medicines known as benzodiazepines also may be used to help with sleep and reduce anxiety symptoms. Examples include alprazolam (Xanax), clonazepam (Klonopin), diazepam (Valium), and lorazepam (Ativan). These medicines can be habit-forming and should not be mixed with alcohol. Possible side effects include drowsiness, dizziness, and memory loss.

When patients are in a depressed state, the usual antidepressant medications have been shown to be helpful. However, it is important for the patient to also be on a mood stabilizer so that the antidepressant medication does not induce a manic state.

Various forms of psychotherapy are also important components of a treatment plan for patients with bipolar disorder. These therapies may take the form of cognitive behavioral therapy (CBT), psychoeducation, and family-focused therapy. Systematic reviews of various forms of psychotherapy for bipolar disorder suggest that family interpersonal therapy (which aims to change problematic relationship patterns) and systematic care seem most effective in preventing recurrences of episodes when the therapies are started after an acute episode. Systematic care involves the use of structured group psychoeducation, telephone monitoring of symptoms and medication adherence, feedback to treating mental health providers, facilitation of follow-up care, and outreach and crisis intervention as needed.

DID YOU KNOW?

Creative people have higher rates of manic-depressive illness compared with people in the general population. The list of eminent artists, musicians, and writers with the illness includes the following:

✓ Samuel Taylor Coleridge

✓ Charles Dickens

✓ Emily Dickinson

✓ William Faulkner

✓ Paul Gauguin

✓ Ernest Hemingway

✓ Charles Ives

✓ Eugene O'Neill

✓ Jackson Pollock

✓ Sergei Rachmaninoff

✓ Mark Rothko

✓ Virginia Woolf

ALTERNATIVE AND SELF-HELP STRATEGIES

Some of the psychotherapy approaches used for treating the illness can be done without a therapist. For example, CBT is available online and has been shown to be effective. For more serious forms of the condition, however, it is recommended that these self-help approaches complement work with a mental health professional.

Changes in dietary habits can help reduce symptoms. People who consume a Mediterranean-style diet consisting of vegetables, fruit, lean meat, fish, and whole grains have fewer mood symptoms in general, according to population-based studies. By contrast, those who eat a "Western diet" that includes processed meats, pizza, chocolate, sweets, soft drinks, margarine, French fries, beer, coffee, cake, and ice cream have greater mood symptoms. Other dietary adjustments can help reduce symptoms, such as decreasing caffeine and alcohol consumption. Occasionally, food allergies can contribute to symptoms, so making sure the patient does not have specific food allergies makes sense.

Physical exercise can reduce symptoms of depression and help with insomnia, fatigue, and other physical symptoms. Mindfulness meditation therapies can also help patients relax and alter their perception of negative thoughts so they simply view them as thoughts and words that come and go and have minimal value. Several herbal supplements may be helpful, including chamomile, kava, winter cherry, valerian root, St. John's wort, passionflower, and others. The scientific evidence supporting their effectiveness, however, is limited.

CHAPTER 8

Dreading Dark Days of Winter: Seasonal Depression

*The winding down of summer puts
me in a heavy philosophical mood.*
—Robert Fulghum

CHARLIE ALWAYS GOT A little down when summer was over and school started in the fall. He figured it was just the disappointment of summer vacation ending and having to get back into the grind of doing homework and going to classes.

He was out of school now and starting his career in the insurance business, yet he still found himself dragging around during the autumn months. He especially felt it in the mornings—it was a struggle to get himself out of bed, and his usual cup of coffee just didn't give him the pep it used to.

His girlfriend, Taylor, said that maybe he had this thing called *SAD*—she had read about in a magazine. Charlie quipped that he already knew he was sad, so what was she talking about? Taylor said that *SAD* stood for *seasonal affective disorder*, and it meant that some people get depressed when the days get shorter in the fall and winter and they are exposed to less sunlight.

Charlie thought it sounded suspicious, but he agreed to look into it. He found a doctor who had experience with SAD and learned that all he needed to do for treatment was sit in front of a special lamp for about a half hour each day.

Despite his continuing skepticism, Charlie gave it a try. In just under a week, he was convinced that SAD was a real thing, and he was delighted that he felt like his old self again—and he didn't have to wait until spring to get back to normal.

During the course of any day, most people experience a range of mild emotional fluctuations from sadness to happiness, but sometimes, those sad feelings get more intense and last longer than we'd like. Such depressive episodes can take many forms, and it is important to determine what leads to a particular type of depression in order to figure out the most effective treatment. Stress may contribute to any mood swing, but many people also have a genetic susceptibility as well as various biological predispositions that make them more sensitive to environmental changes.

During the past few decades, neuroscientists have focused on a particular form of depression that varies according to the season of the year that appears to be triggered by reduced exposure to sunlight during the shorter days of fall and winter. This phenomenon is often referred to as winter depression, but if the mood swings are severe enough to interfere with everyday life, then the condition is called seasonal affective disorder, which has the apt acronym of SAD.

DIAGNOSING SAD

Sometimes people like Charlie notice that when fall and winter come around, they feel a bit down in the dumps. They may attribute the mood swing to their youthful disappointment over summer vacation ending and the school year beginning, making them say goodbye to those relaxing, warm, sunny days.

Many of these people fail to realize that their seasonal mood dip may be due to briefer exposure to sunlight during those shorter days that came with fall and winter. They may be suffering from winter depression or SAD, and their low moods have more to do with the effect of less light exposure on their brain neurotransmitters.

DO YOU HAVE SAD?

The fifth edition of the American Psychiatrist Association's *Diagnostic and Statistical Manual of Mental Disorders* (DSM-5) describes SAD as a form of recurrent major depressive disorder with a seasonal pattern: the depressive episodes usually occur during the fall and winter and remit during spring and summer. These episodes meet the criteria for a major depressive disorder if the patient experiences five or more of the following symptoms over two weeks or more. One of the symptoms must be either a depressed mood or a loss of interest.

☐ Depressed mood (sadness, hopelessness, tears) throughout the day

☐ Decreased interest or pleasure in most activities

☐ Significant weight loss or weight gain or decrease or increase in appetite

☐ Insomnia or increased sleep

☐ Agitation or slowed thinking or behavior

☐ Fatigue or energy loss

☐ Feeling worthless or inappropriately guilty

☐ Indecisiveness or diminished concentration

☐ Recurrent thoughts of death or suicide

If these symptoms interfere with everyday life and a medical illness is not the cause, then SAD is the diagnosis. "Winter blues" show similar but less severe symptoms that do not interfere with daily functioning.

For some time, researchers had reported greater symptoms of depression and lower energy levels during the winter in people who lived a far distance from the equator—geographic regions where daytime sunlight hours are briefer during the winter compared to regions closer to the equator. In the 1980s, South African physician Norman Rosenthal first recognized SAD as a treatable condition. When Dr. Rosenthal moved to the US, he noticed that his own productivity was lower during the winter months and improved when spring arrived. In collaborations with Drs. Al Lewy and Tom Wehr at the National Institutes of Health, the team linked SAD to the body's internal clock, which is cued by sunlight (i.e., circadian rhythms) and a hormone called melatonin, which is suppressed by light exposure to the eye.

Winter blues and SAD differ in that the former is a milder condition that usually improves with greater light exposure and physical activity. By contrast, the treatment of SAD may require the use of antidepressants, psychotherapy, and bright-light therapy.

Women have a fourfold greater risk for developing these conditions compared with men, and the risk for anyone increases according to the distance of their residence from the equator. In fact, residents of Alaska have a 10 percent risk for developing SAD, while the risk for Floridians is only 1 percent. Older people have a lower risk than do younger people, and if you have a close relative with SAD, your own risk is higher.

BRAIN EFFECTS OF LIGHT EXPOSURE

Certain neurotransmitters or brain messengers that control mood appear to be the underlying problem causing SAD. Research has demonstrated that during the winter, SAD patients have higher levels of a brain protein called SERT, which transports the mood-stabilizing neurotransmitter serotonin. Summer sunlight lowers SERT levels, but fewer hours of sunlight during the fall and winter increase SERT levels, which in turn lowers serotonin activity. Patients with SAD also produce too much melatonin, a sleep-inducing hormone stimulated by darkness. Many people use melatonin supplements to help their insomnia and jet-lag symptoms. Patients with SAD have too much melatonin, which leads to daytime lethargy. Functional MRI scans before and after bright-light therapy show that the light therapy changes the volunteer's risk-taking behavior and brain neural activity. Light exposure increases risk-taking in proportion to the amount of light exposure, and risk-taking behavior increases along with levels of neural activity in the brain's striatum. This is a brain area that controls current and anticipated rewards. The risk-taking behavior in this study was a gambling task, which may explain why gambling casinos are so well lit twenty-four hours a day. The light may encourage people to take more risks and stay longer at the poker, craps, and blackjack tables.

CONVENTIONAL TREATMENTS THAT WORK

Antidepressant medicines have been shown to be effective in treating SAD. Because the condition is associated with an imbalance of the mood-altering neurotransmitter serotonin in the brain, the selective serotonin reuptake inhibitors (SSRIs) will improve symptoms, and such medicines are sometimes as effective as light therapy. For patients with more severe symptoms, antidepressants are inadequate in controlling symptoms entirely.

For such patients, bright-light therapy or phototherapy should be used to augment the effects of antidepressants. Specially manufactured light boxes that emit full-spectrum light comparable in intensity to direct sunlight are used for this purpose. Symptom relief is often achieved by sitting in front of a light box for twenty minutes to an hour at the beginning of each day.

Many patients will continue the light therapy from early fall until the end of winter. The light boxes provide exposure that is twenty times greater than ordinary indoor lighting while filtering out ultraviolet rays. Possible side effects include eyestrain, headaches, irritability, and heightened risk for age-related macular degeneration. Light therapy may also help patients with other forms of depression. Brain imaging studies show that phototherapy lowers the binding of the serotonin transporter in the brain's frontal lobe.

Sunlight exposure elevates the body's vitamin D levels, and some people who spend little time outdoors may have a vitamin D deficiency, which can heighten their risk for symptoms of depression. A doctor can check for blood levels, and if low, the patient should take daily vitamin D supplements to improve symptoms.

Talking with a professional counselor or therapist or joining a support group with other people who have winter blues or SAD can assist patients in coping better with their symptoms. Cognitive behavioral therapy (CBT) has been shown to help people get a better handle on their problems and reduce their negative thinking patterns. The benefits of CBT in patients with winter blues or SAD may be comparable to those from daily light therapy.

SELF-HELP AND ALTERNATIVE STRATEGIES FOR WINTER BLUES AND SAD

Some of the following strategies also may help ward off or prevent negative seasonal emotions.

- *Light up your space.* Not everyone needs a fancy light box to brighten up their immediate environment. When you get up in the morning, open the window shades or curtains and close them in the evening *after* the sun sets. Trim trees that may be blocking windows to let in more light. Even on cloudy days, you'll benefit from the sunlight that penetrates the cloud cover.

- *Readjust your schedule.* When daylight saving ends, go to bed and get up earlier to optimize your light exposure. Your adjusted routine will assist your body's internal clock to reset and promote restful sleep at night, which can boost your mood during the day.

- *Play outside.* Whenever possible, go outside to soak in some natural sunlight. Outdoor physical exercise is great for your brain health in general, and studies indicate exercising in brightly lit areas has superior mood benefits compared with workouts in darker spaces.

- *Up your bulb wattage.* Indoor lighting has less of a mood-boosting benefit than outdoor light, but using higher-wattage light bulbs certainly won't hurt your disposition. It will also reduce eyestrain from reading and computer use.

- *Reduce stress.* Meditation, deep-breathing exercises, tai chi, and other relaxation techniques have been shown to benefit mood in many different types of depression. Spending time with friends, especially empathic ones, will help you put your worries into perspective. Taking a walk or any form of aerobic conditioning with friends will increase mood-enhancing endorphins, and you'll have a chance to further lower your stress levels by talking with an empathic companion.

Epilogue

_____

WHETHER YOU EXPERIENCE MILD symptoms of depression or you have more challenging mood changes that make your life difficult, the information in this guide has hopefully helped you better understand your symptoms as well as provided ways to effectively deal with them. In addition to the different types of depression people may experience, those suffering from a variety of other psychiatric conditions may also experience sadness and other symptoms typical of depression. For example, feelings of sadness and guilt can be prominent in people with anxiety disorders, eating disorders, and many other mental health disorders. If you are concerned about any mental symptoms that you or a loved one may be experiencing, talking with your doctor or a mental health professional is an important first step to getting help.

Numerous other resources are available in the community to help people cope with depressive symptoms and disorders. Organizations such as the Anxiety and Depression Association of America (www.adaa.org), the American Psychiatric Association (www.psychiatry.org), the American Psychological Association (www.apa.org), and the National Institute of Mental Health (www.nimh.nih.gov) have websites with information about these conditions and strategies for getting help and referrals. The good news is that most forms of depression disorder do respond to treatment once accurately diagnosed. The sooner you get help, the sooner you can enjoy your life without the hindrance of the sometimes annoying and other times debilitating symptoms of depression.

Acknowledgments

WE ARE GRATEFUL TO our colleagues, friends, and family members who provided their encouragement and input while we wrote this book, including our daughter Rachel and our son Harrison. We also appreciate the support and guidance of our longtime agent and friend, Sandra Dijkstra and her entire team, as well as Mary Glenn at Humanix Books.

Gary Small, MD, and Gigi Vorgan

Note: *Many stories and examples contained in this book are composite accounts based on the experiences of several individuals and do not represent any one person or group of people. Similarities to any one person or persons are coincidental and unintentional. Readers may wish to talk with their doctor before starting any exercise or diet program.*

Bibliography

PREFACE

American Psychiatric Association. "New Poll: COVID-19 Impacting Mental Well-Being: Americans Feeling Anxious, Especially for Loved Ones; Older Adults Are Less Anxious." APA Newsroom, Mar. 25, 2020. https://www.psychiatry.org/newsroom/news-releases/new-poll-covid-19-impacting-mental-well-being-americans-feeling-anxious-especially-for-loved-ones-older-adults-are-less-anxious.

National Institute of Mental Health. "Suicide." NIH Mental Health Information, accessed Feb. 1, 2021. https://www.nimh.nih.gov/health/statistics/suicide.shtml.

CHAPTER 1: WHAT IS DEPRESSION
AND DO YOU HAVE IT?

Albert, P. R. "Why Is Depression More Prevalent in Women?" *J Psychiatry Neurosci* 40, no. 4 (Jul. 2015): 219–21. DOI: 10.1503/jpn.150205.

American Psychiatric Association. *Diagnostic and Statistical Manual of Mental Disorders.* 5th ed. Arlington, VA: American Psychiatric Publishing, 2013.

Beck, A. T., et al. "Psychometric Properties of the Beck Depression Inventory: Twenty-Five Years of Evaluation." *Clin Psychol Rev* 8 (1988): 77–100.

Belvederi Murri, M., et al. "Physical Exercise in Major Depression: Reducing the Mortality Gap While Improving Clinical Outcomes." *Front Psychiatry* 9 (2018): 762. DOI: 10.3389/fpsyt.2018.00762.

Charlson, F. J., et al. "The Contribution of Major Depression to the Global Burden of Ischemic Heart Disease: A Comparative Risk Assessment." *BMC Med* 11, no. 250 (2013). DOI: 10.1186/1741 -7015-11-250.

Cohen-Cole, S. A., and Stoudemire, A. "Major Depression and Physical Illness: Special Considerations in Diagnosis and Biologic Treatment." *Psychiatric Clin North Am* 10 (1987): 1–17.

Cuijpers, P., et al. "Excess Mortality in Depression: A Meta-analysis of Community Studies." *J Affect Dis* 72 (2002): 227–36.

Hammer-Helmich, L., et al. "Functional Impairment
    in Patients with Major Depressive Disorder: The
    2-Year PERFORM Study." *Neuropsychiatr Dis
    Treat* 14 (2018): 239–49.

Hunt, M. G., et al. "No More FOMO: Limiting Social
    Media Decreases Loneliness and Depression."
    J Soc Clin Psychol 37 (2018): 751–68.

Jacka, F. N., et al. "Association of Western and Tra-
    ditional Diets with Depression and Anxiety in
    Women." *Am J Psychiatry* 167 (2010): 305–11.

Janssen, C. W., et al. "Whole-Body Hyperthermia for
    the Treatment of Major Depressive Disorder: A
    Randomized Clinical Trial." *JAMA Psychiatry* 73,
    no. 8 (2016): 789–95.

Li, Y., et al. "Dietary Patterns and Depression Risk: A
    Meta-analysis." *Psychiatry Research* 253 (2017):
    373–82.

Mangiola, F., et al. "Gut Microbiota in Autism and
    Mood Disorders." *J Psychiatry Neurosci World J
    Gastroenterol* 22, no. 1 (Jan. 7, 2016): 361–68.

Martin, C. K., et al. "Effect of Calorie Restriction on
    Mood, Quality of Life, Sleep, and Sexual Func-
    tion in Healthy Nonobese Adults: The CALERIE
    2 Randomized Clinical Trial." *JAMA Intern Med*
    176, no. 6 (Jun. 1, 2016): 743–52.

National Institute of Mental Health. "Major Depres-
    sion." NIH Mental Health Information, accessed
    Feb. 1, 2021. https://www.nimh.nih.gov/health/
    statistics/major-depression.shtml.

Navrady, L. B., et al. "Intelligence and Neuroticism in Relation to Depression and Psychological Distress: Evidence from Two Large Population Cohorts." *Eur Psychiatry* 43 (Jun. 2017): 58–65.

Olfson, M., et al. "Short-Term Suicide Risk after Psychiatric Hospital Discharge." *JAMA Psychiatry* 73 (2016): 1119–26.

Pandya, M., et al. "Where in the Brain Is Depression?" *Curr Psychiatry Rep* 14, no. 6 (Dec. 2012): 634–42.

Pew Research Center. "Social Media Fact Sheet." Jun. 12, 2019. https://www.pewresearch.org/internet/fact-sheet/social-media/.

Pratt, L. A., and Brody, D. J. "Depression in the U.S. Household Population, 2009–2012." NCHS Data Brief no. 172, Dec. 2014. https://www.cdc.gov/nchs/data/databriefs/db172.pdf.

Schonfeld, W. H., et al. "The Functioning and Well-Being of Patients with Unrecognized Anxiety Disorders and Major Depressive Disorder." *J Affective Disorders* 43 (1997): 105–19.

Shadrina, E., et al. "Genetics Factors in Major Depression Disease." *Front Psychiatry* 9 (2018): 334. DOI: 10.cc89/fpsyt.2018.00334.

Small, G., and Vorgan, G. *SNAP! Change Your Personality in 30 Days*. New York: Humanix, 2018.

Tang, S., et al. "Abnormal Amygdala Resting-State Functional Connectivity in Adults and Adolescents with Major Depressive Disorder: A Comparative Meta-analysis." *EBioMedicine* 36 (Oct. 2018): 436–45.

Thielke, S. M., et al. "Prevalence, Incidence, and Persistence of Major Depressive Symptoms in the Cardiovascular Health Study." *Aging Ment Health* 14, no. 2 (Mar. 2010): 168–76.

Wang, J., et al. "Prevalence of Depression and Depressive Symptoms among Outpatients: A Systematic Review and Meta-analysis." *BMJ Open* 7, no. 8 (2017): e017173. DOI: 10.1136/bmjopen-2017-017173.

Zung, W. W. "A Self-Rating Depression Scale." *Arch Gen Psychiatry* 12 (1965): 63–70.

CHAPTER 2: DO-IT-YOURSELF STRATEGIES FOR IMPROVING MOOD

Choi, K. W., et al. "Assessment of Bidirectional Relationships between Physical Activity and Depression among Adults: A 2-Sample Mendelian Randomization Study." *JAMA Psychiatry* 76, no. 4 (2019): 399–408.

Desai, R., et al. "Effects of Yoga on Brain Waves and Structural Activation: A Review." *Complement Ther Clin Pract* 21 (2015): 112–18.

Fiona, S., et al. "International Tables of Glycemic Index and Glycemic Load Values." *Diabetes Care* 31 (2008): 2281–83.

Harvard Health Publishing. "Calories Burned in 30 Minutes for People of Three Different Weights."

Last updated Aug. 13, 2018. http://www.health
.harvard.edu/diet-and-weight-loss/calories-burned
-in-30-minutes-of-leisure-and-routine-activities.

Jacka, F. N., et al. "Association of Western and Traditional Diets with Depression and Anxiety in
Women." *Am J Psychiatry* 167 (2010): 305–11.

Josefien, J. F., et al. "The Effects of Meditation, Yoga,
and Mindfulness on Depression, Anxiety, and
Stress in Tertiary Education Students: A Meta-
analysis." *Front Psychiatry* 10 (2019): 193. DOI:
10.3389/fpsyt.2019.00193.

Last, N., et al. "The Effects of Meditation on Grey Matter Atrophy and Neurodegeneration: A Systematic
Review." *J Alzheimers Dis* 56 (2017): 275–86.

Li, L., et al. "Insomnia and the Risk of Depression:
A Meta-analysis of Prospective Cohort Studies."
BMC Psychiatry 16, no. 375 (2016). DOI: 10.1186/
s12888-016-1075-3.

Low Dog, T. "The Role of Nutrition in Mental Health."
Altern Ther Health Med 16 (2010): 42–46.

Marx, W., et al. "Nutritional Psychiatry: The Present
State of the Evidence." *Proc Nutr Soc* 76, no. 4 (Nov.
2017): 427–36. DOI: 10.1017/S0029665117002026.

Morgan, A. J., and Jorm, A. F. "Self-Help Interventions
for Depressive Disorders and Depressive Symptoms: A Systematic Review." *Ann Gen Psychiatry* 7
(2008): 13. DOI: 10.1186/1744-859X-7-13.

National Institute for Health and Clinical Excel-
lence (NICE). *Computerised Cognitive Behaviour*

Therapy for Depression and Anxiety (Review of Technology Appraisal 51). London: NICE, 2006.

Saeed, S. A., et al. "Depression and Anxiety Disorders: Benefits of Exercise, Yoga, and Meditation." *Am Fam Physician* 99, no. 10 (May 15, 2019): 620–27.

Seabrook, E. M., et al. "Social Networking Sites, Depression, and Anxiety: A Systematic Review." *JMIR Ment Health* 3, no. 4 (Nov. 2016): e50.

Strauss, C., et al. "Mindfulness-Based Interventions for People Diagnosed with a Current Episode of an Anxiety or Depressive Disorder: A Meta-analysis of Randomised Controlled Trials." *PLOS One* 9, no. 4 (2014): e96110. DOI: 10.1371/journal.pone.0096110.

Webb, C. A., et al. "Internet-Based Cognitive Behavioral Therapy for Depression: Current Progress & Future Directions." *Harv Rev Psychiatry* 25, no. 3 (May–Jun. 2017): 114–22.

CHAPTER 3: CONVENTIONAL DEPRESSION TREATMENTS THAT WORK

Andrade, C. "Ketamine for Depression, 1: Clinical Summary of Issues Related to Efficacy, Adverse Effects, and Mechanism of Action." *J Clin Psychiatry* 78, no. 4 (2017): E415–19.

Antony, M. M., and Stein, M. B. *Oxford Handbook of Anxiety and Related Disorders*. Oxford: Oxford University Press, 2008.

A-Tiak, J. G., et al. "A Meta-analysis of the Efficacy of Acceptance and Commitment Therapy for Clinically Relevant Mental and Physical Health Problems." *Psychother Psychosom* 84, no. 1 (2015): 30–36. DOI: 10.1159/000365764.

Briggs, R., et al. "What Is the Prevalence of Untreated Depression and Death Ideation in Older People? Data from the Irish Longitudinal Study on Aging." *Int Psychogeriatr* 30, no. 9 (Sep. 2018): 1393–1401.

Bystritsky, A., et al. "Current Diagnosis and Treatment of Anxiety Disorders." *Pharmacy and Therapeutics* 38 (2013): 41–44.

Carhart-Harris, R. L., et al. "Psilocybin with Psychological Support for Treatment-Resistant Depression: Six-Month Follow-Up." *Psychopharmacol* 235 (2018): 399–408.

Chapman, A. L. "Dialectical Behavior Therapy: Current Indications and Unique Elements." *Psychiatry (Edgmont)* 3, no. 9 (Sep. 2006): 62–68.

Cook, I. A., et al. "Neuromodulation for Depression: Invasive and Noninvasive (Deep Brain Stimulation, Transcranial Magnetic Stimulation, Trigeminal Nerve Stimulation)." *Neurosurg Clin N Am* 25, no. 1 (Jan. 2014): 103–16.

Fredette, C., et al. "Using Hypnosis in the Treatment of Anxiety Disorders: Pros and Cons." In *New Insights into Anxiety Disorders*, edited by F. Durbano. IntechOpen, Mar. 20, 2013. DOI: 10.5772/53768.

Gelenberg, A. J. "A Review of the Current Guidelines for Depression Treatment." *J Clin Psychiatry* 71, no. 7 (Jul. 2010): e15. DOI: 10.4088/JCP.9078tx1c.

Hofmann, S. G., et al. "The Efficacy of Cognitive Behavioral Therapy: A Review of Meta-analyses." *Cognitive Therapy and Research* 36 (2012): 427–40.

Hofmann, S. T., et al. "The Effect of Mindfulness-Based Therapy on Anxiety and Depression: A Meta-analytic Review." *J Consult Clin Psychol* 78 (2010): 169–83.

Kerner, N., and Prudic, J. "Current Electroconvulsive Therapy Practice and Research in the Geriatric Population." *Neuropsychiatry (London)* 4, no. 1 (Feb. 2014): 33–54.

Levine, P. A., and Crane-Godreau, M. A. "Somatic Experiencing: Using Interoception and Proprioception as Core Elements of Trauma Therapy." *Front Psychol*, Feb. 4, 2015.

Ogawa, Y., et al. "Antidepressants plus Benzodiazepines for Adults with Major Depression." *Cochrane Database Syst Rev* 6, no. 6 (Jun. 3, 2019): CD001026. DOI: 10.1002/14651858.CD001026.pub2.

Payne, P., et al. "Somatic Experiencing: Using Interoception and Proprioception as Core Elements of Trauma Therapy." *Front Psychol* 6 (Feb. 4, 2015): 93. DOI: 10.3389/fpsyg.2015.00093. eCollection 2015.

Stahl, S. M. *Essential Psychopharmacology of Depression and Bipolar Disorder.* Cambridge, MA: Cambridge University Press, 2000.

Swedish Council on Health Technology Assessment. "Treatment of Anxiety Disorders: A Systematic Review." SBU Yellow Report no. 171/1+2, Nov. 2005.

Thomaes, K., et al. "Degrading Traumatic Memories with Eye Movements: A Pilot Functional MRI Study in PTSD." *Eur J Psychotraumatol* 7 (Nov. 29, 2016): 31371. DOI: 10.3402/ejpt.v7.31371.

Walser, R. D., et al. "Training in and Implementation of Acceptance and Commitment Therapy for Depression in the Veterans Health Administration: Therapist and Patient Outcomes." *Behaviour Research and Therapy* 51 (2013): 555–63.

Wright, B. M. "Augmentation with Atypical Antipsychotics for Depression: A Review of Evidence-Based Support from the Medical Literature." *Pharmacotherapy* 33 (2013): 344–59.

CHAPTER 4: ALTERNATIVE THERAPIES

Bai, S., et al. "Efficacy and Safety of Anti-inflammatory Agents for the Treatment of Major Depressive Disorder: A Systematic Review and Meta-analysis of Randomised Controlled Trials." *J Neurol Neurosurg Psychiatry* 91, no. 1 (Jan. 2020): 21–32.

Banerjee, S., and Argáez, C. *Neurofeedback and Bio-feedback for Mood and Anxiety Disorders: A Review of Clinical Effectiveness and Guidelines.* CADTH Rapid Response Reports, Nov. 13, 2017.

Bennabi, D., and Haffen, E. "Transcranial Direct Current Stimulation (tDCS): A Promising Treatment for Major Depressive Disorder?" *Brain Sci* 8, no. 5 (May 2018): 81.

Berk, M., et al. "Effect of Aspirin vs Placebo on the Prevention of Depression in Older People: A Randomized Clinical Trial." *JAMA Psychiatry* 77, no. 10 (2020). DOI: 10.1001/jamapsychiatry.2020.1214.

Davidson, J. R., et al. "Homeopathic Treatments in Psychiatry: A Systematic Review of Randomized Placebo-Controlled Studies." *J Clin Psychiatry* 72 (2011): 795–805.

D'Urso, G., et al. "Transcranial Direct Current Stimulation for Obsessive-Compulsive Disorder: A Randomized, Controlled, Partial Cover Trial." *Depress Anxiety* 33 (2016): 1132–40.

Fedotova, J., et al. "Therapeutical Strategies for Anxiety and Anxiety-like Disorders Using Plant-Derived Natural Compounds and Plant Extracts." *Biomed Pharmacother* 95 (2017): 437–46.

Field, T. "Massage Therapy Research Review." *Complement Ther Clin Pract* 20 (2014): 224–29.

Fomenko, A., et al. "Low-Intensity Ultrasound Neuromodulation: An Overview of Mechanisms and

Emerging Human Applications." *Brain Stimul* 11, no. 6 (2018): 1209–17.

Freeman, M. P., et al. "Complementary and Alternative Medicine in Major Depressive Disorder: The American Psychiatric Association Task Force Report." *J Clin Psychiatry* 71 (2010): 669–81.

Fusar Poli, L., et al. "Curcumin for Depression: A Meta-analysis." *Crit Rev Food Sci Nutr* (Aug. 19, 2019): 1–11.

Huang, R., et al. "Effect of Probiotics on Depression: A Systematic Review and Meta-analysis of Randomized Controlled Trials." *Nutrients* 8, no. 8 (Aug. 6, 2016): 483. DOI: 10.3390/nu8080483.

Iannone, A. "Transcranial Magnetic Stimulation and Transcranial Direct Current Stimulation Appear to Be Safe Neuromodulatory Techniques Useful in the Treatment of Anxiety Disorders and Other Neuropsychiatric Disorders." *Arq Neuropsiquiatr* 74 (2016): 829–35.

Janssen, C. W., et al. "Whole-Body Hyperthermia for the Treatment of Major Depressive Disorder: A Randomized Clinical Trial." *JAMA Psychiatry* 73, no. 8 (2016): 789–95.

Joyce, J., and Herbison, G. P. "Reiki for Depression and Anxiety." *Cochrane Database Syst Rev*, no. 4 (Apr. 3, 2015): CD006833. DOI: 10.1002/14651858 .CD006833.pub2.

Kessler, R. C., et al. "The Use of Complementary and Alternative Therapies to Treat Anxiety and

Depression in the United States." *Am J Psychiatry* 158 (2001): 289–94.

Lakhan, S. E., and Vieira, K. F. "Nutritional and Herbal Supplements for Anxiety and Anxiety-Related Disorders: Systematic Review." *Nutrition Journal* 9 (2010): 42. http://www.nutritionj.com/content/9/1/42.

Lebowitz, K. R., et al. "Effects of Humor and Laughter on Psychological Functioning, Quality of Life, Health Status, and Pulmonary Functioning among Patients with Chronic Obstructive Pulmonary Disease: A Preliminary Investigation." *Heart Lung* 40 (2011): 310–19.

Marzbani, H., et al. "Neurofeedback: A Comprehensive Review on System Design, Methodology and Clinical Applications." *Basic Clin Neurosci* 7 (2016): 143–58.

Mizrachi Zer-Aviv, T., et al. "Cannabinoids and Post-traumatic Stress Disorder: Clinical and Preclinical Evidence for Treatment and Prevention." *Behav Pharmacol* 27 (2016): 561–69.

Park, C., et al. "Probiotics for the Treatment of Depressive Symptoms: An Anti-inflammatory Mechanism?" *Brain Behav Immun* 73 (Oct. 2018): 115–24.

Pilkington, K. "Acupuncture Therapy for Psychiatric Illness." *Int Rev Neurobiol* 111 (2013): 197–216.

Ravindran, A. V., et al. "Canadian Network for Mood and Anxiety Treatments (CANMAT) 2016 Clinical

Guidelines for the Management of Adults with Major Depressive Disorder: Section 5. Complementary and Alternative Medicine Treatments." *Can J Psychiatry* 61, no. 9 (Sep. 2016): 576–87.

Schmidt, P. J., et al. "Dehydroepiandrosterone Monotherapy in Midlife-Onset Major and Minor Depression." *Arch Gen Psychiatry* 62 (2005): 154–62.

Veronese, N., et al. "Acetyl-L-Carnitine Supplementation and the Treatment of Depressive Symptoms: A Systematic Review and Meta-analysis." *Psychosom Med* 80, no. 2 (Feb./Mar. 2018): 154–59.

CHAPTER 5: BLAHS WITH A CAUSE: SITUATIONAL DEPRESSION

American Psychiatric Association. *Diagnostic and Statistical Manual of Mental Disorders*. 5th ed. Arlington, VA: American Psychiatric Publishing, 2013.

Arends, I., et al. "Interventions to Facilitate Return to Work in Adults with Adjustment Disorders." *Cochrane Database Syst Rev* 12 (2012): CD006389.

Domhardt, M., and Baumeister, H. "Psychotherapy of Adjustment Disorders: Current State and Future Directions." *World J Biol Psychiatry* 19 (2018, sup1): S21–S35.

Fernández, A., et al. "Adjustment Disorders in Primary Care: Prevalence, Recognition and Use of Services." *Br J Psychiatry* 201 (2012): 137–42.

Firth, J., et al. "The Efficacy and Safety of Nutrient Supplements in the Treatment of Mental Disorders: A Meta-review of Meta-analyses of Randomized Controlled Trials." *World Psychiatry* 18, no. 3 (Oct. 2019): 308–24.

Maercker, A., et al. "Adjustment Disorders Are Uniquely Suited for eHealth Interventions: Concept and Case Study." *JMIR Ment Health* 2, no. 2 (Apr.–Jun. 2015): e15. DOI: 10.2196/mental .4157.

Maercker, A., and Lorenz, L. "Adjustment Disorder Diagnosis: Improving Clinical Utility." *World J Biol Psychiatry* 19 (2018, sup1): S3–S13.

Mitchell, A. J., et al. "Prevalence and Predictors of Post-stroke Mood Disorders: A Meta-analysis and Meta-regression of Depression, Anxiety and Adjustment Disorder." *Gen Hosp Psychiatry* 47 (2017): 48–60.

CHAPTER 6: BLUES THAT COME AND GO: CLINICAL DEPRESSION

American Psychiatric Association. *Diagnostic and Statistical Manual of Mental Disorders.* 5th ed.

Arlington, VA: American Psychiatric Publishing, 2013.

Gartlehner, G., et al. "Pharmacological and Nonpharmacological Treatments for Major Depressive Disorder: Review of Systematic Reviews." *BMJ Open* 7, no. 6 (Jun. 14, 2017): e014912.

Goodwin, G. M. "Depression and Associated Physical Diseases and Symptoms." *Dialogues Clin Neurosci* 8, no. 2 (Jun. 2006): 259–65.

Hasin, D. S., et al. "Epidemiology of Adult DSM-5 Major Depressive Disorder and Its Specifiers in the United States." *JAMA Psychiatry* 75, no. 4 (2018): 336–46.

Park, C., et al. "Predicting Antidepressant Response Using Early Changes in Cognition: A Systematic Review." *Behavioural Brain Research* 353 (2018): 154–60.

Small, G. W. "Differential Diagnoses and Assessment of Depression in Elderly Patients." *J Clin Psychiatry* 70 (2009): e47.

CHAPTER 7: SWINGING HIGH AND LOW: MANIC DEPRESSION

Culpepper, L. "The Diagnosis and Treatment of Bipolar Disorder: Decision-Making in Primary Care." *Prim Care Companion CNS Disord* 16, no. 3 (2014): PCC.13r01609. DOI: 10.4088/PCC.13r01609.

Goodwin, G. M., et al. "Evidence-Based Guidelines for Treating Bipolar Disorder: Revised Third Edition Recommendations from the British Association for Psychopharmacology." *Psychopharmacol* 30 (2016): 495–553.

Harrison, P. J., et al. "Innovative Approaches to Bipolar Disorder and Its Treatment." *Ann N Y Acad Sci* 1366, no. 1 (Feb. 2016): 76–89.

Johnson, S. L., et al. "Creativity and Bipolar Disorder: Touched by Fire or Burning with Questions?" *Clin Psychol Rev* 32 (2012): 1–12.

Miklowitz, D. J. "Adjunctive Psychotherapy for Bipolar Disorder: State of the Evidence." *Am J Psychiatry* 165 (2008): 1408–19.

CHAPTER 8: DREADING DARK DAYS OF WINTER: SEASONAL DEPRESSION

American Psychiatric Association. *Diagnostic and Statistical Manual of Mental Disorders*. 5th ed. Arlington, VA: American Psychiatric Publishing, 2013.

Levitan, R. D. "The Chronobiology and Neurobiology of Winter Seasonal Affective Disorder." *Dialogues Clin Neurosci* 9 (2007): 315–24.

Macoveanu, J., et al. "Bright-Light Intervention Induces a Dose-Dependent Increase in Striatal Response to Risk in Healthy Volunteers." *Neuroimage* 139 (2016): 37–43.

Meesters, Y., and Gordijn, M. C. M. "Seasonal Affec-
    tive Disorder, Winter Type: Current Insights and
    Treatment Options." *Psychol Res Behav Manag* 9
    (2016): 317–27.

Melrose, S. "Seasonal Affective Disorder: An Over-
    view of Assessment and Treatment Approaches."
    Depress Res Treat 2015 (2015): 178564. DOI:
    10.1155/2015/178564.

Index

Page numbers in *italics* refer to figures.

About the Authors

Gary Small, MD, and **Gigi Vorgan** are the authors of the *New York Times* bestseller *The Memory Bible* as well as *The Memory Prescription, The Longevity Bible, iBrain, The Other Side of the Couch, The Alzheimer's Prevention Program, 2 Weeks to a Younger Brain, SNAP! Change Your Personality in 30 Days, The Small Guide to Anxiety,* and *The Small Guide to Alzheimer's Disease.* Dr. Small is chair of psychiatry at Hackensack University Medical Center and physician in chief for behavioral health at Hackensack Meridian Health, New Jersey's largest and most comprehensive health care network. Prior to joining Hackensack Meridian Health, Small was a professor of psychiatry and aging at the David Geffen School of Medicine at UCLA, director of the Division of Geriatric Psychiatry at the Semel Institute, and director of the UCLA Longevity Center. Named one of the world's top fifty innovators in science and technology by *Scientific American*, he has appeared frequently on *Today*, *Good Morning America*, PBS, and CNN and lectures throughout the world. In addition to working as coauthor with her husband Dr. Small, Ms. Vorgan has written feature films and television. She and Dr. Small live together in Weehawken, New Jersey.

For more information on their books and Dr. Small's appearances, visit DrGarySmall.com.

RateMyMemory

Powered by newsmax health

Normal Forgetfulness?
Something More Serious?

You forget things — names of people, where you parked your car, the place you put an important document, and so much more. Some experts tell you to dismiss these episodes.

"Not so fast," say the editors of Newsmax Health, and publishers of *The Mind Health Report*.

The experts at Newsmax Health say that most age-related memory issues are normal but sometimes can be a warning sign of future cognitive decline.

Now Newsmax Health has created the online **RateMyMemory Test** — allowing you to easily assess your memory strength in just a matter of minutes.

It's time to begin your journey of making sure your brain stays healthy and young! **It takes just 2 minutes!**

Test Your Memory Today:
MemoryRate.com/Guide

Simple **Heart Test**

Powered by Newsmaxhealth.com

FACT:

▶ Nearly half of those who die from heart attacks each year never showed prior symptoms of heart disease.

▶ If you suffer cardiac arrest outside of a hospital, you have just a 7% chance of survival.

Don't be caught off guard. Know your risk now.

TAKE THE TEST NOW ...

Renowned cardiologist **Dr. Chauncey Crandall** has partnered with **Newsmaxhealth.com** to create a simple, easy-to-complete, online test that will help you understand your heart attack risk factors. Dr. Crandall is the author of the #1 best-seller *The Simple Heart Cure: The 90-Day Program to Stop and Reverse Heart Disease.*

Take Dr. Crandall's Simple Heart Test — it takes just 2 minutes or less to complete — it could save your life!

Discover your risk now.

- **Where you score on our unique heart disease risk scale**
- Which of your lifestyle habits really protect your heart
- **The true role your height and weight play in heart attack risk**
- Little-known conditions that impact heart health
- **Plus much more!**

SimpleHeartTest.com/Guide